At Issue

| Vaping

Other Books in the At Issue Series

At Issue

| Vaping

Andrew Karpan, Book Editor

GREENHAVEN
PUBLISHING

Published in 2020 by Greenhaven Publishing, LLC
353 3rd Avenue, Suite 255, New York, NY 10010

Articles in Greenhaven Publishing anthologies are often edited for length to meet page
requirements. In addition, original titles of these works are changed to clearly present
the main thesis and to explicitly indicate the author's opinion. Every effort is made to
ensure that Greenhaven Publishing accurately reflects the original intent of the authors.
Every effort has been made to trace the owners of the copyrighted material.

Cover image: Sefa Karacan/Anadolu Agency/Getty Images

Library of Congress Cataloging-in-Publication Data

Names: Karpan, Andrew, editor.
Title: Vaping / Andrew Karpan, book editor, [compiling editor].
Other titles: At issue
Description: First edition. | New York : Greenhaven Publishing, [2020] |
Series: At issue | Includes bibliographical references and index. | Audience: Grades 9-
12.
Identifiers: LCCN 2018059647| ISBN 9781534505124 (library bound) | ISBN
9781534505131 (pbk.)
Subjects: LCSH: Vaping—Juvenile literature. | Electronic
cigarettes—Juvenile literature. | Smoking—Health aspects—Juvenile
literature. | Youth—Tobacco use—Juvenile literature.
Classification: LCC HV5748 .V37 2019 | DDC 362.29/6—dc23
LC record available at https://lccn.loc.gov/2018059647

Manufactured in the United States of America

Website: http://greenhavenpublishing.com

Contents

Introduction

In a lawsuit filed in October 2018, the mother of a high school student in Florida alleged that the social media pages run by Juul Labs, Inc. both target minors and hide exactly how much nicotine the popular—and often flavored—plastic pods of e-liquid, or "vape juice," contains.[1] The abundance of flavors was also doing the company a world of good among teenagers. Mint, in particular, was the favorite flavor of the student whose mother instigated legal action. The next month, the *New York Times* printed a darker story. Matt Murphy, a 17-year-old in Massachusetts who also enjoyed Juul's mint-flavored variety, told the newspaper: "I could not justify the addiction anymore."[2] According to a CDC survey conducted that month, the number of middle and high school students currently vaping was about 3.6 million.[3] Days earlier, Juul announced they'd had enough, shutting down its pages on Facebook and Instagram and suspending sales of most of its flavored e-cigarettes. For the time being, though, it was keeping mint.

Nicotine is an American invention. One of the earliest recorded uses of tobacco leaves, which contain nicotine, was in the remains of a pot designed to hold cut and cured tobacco leaves from around 700 CE in what is now the Mexican state of Campeche. The word "nicotine" comes from the colonizers who would wipe out the Mayan population. Jean Nicot, a French ambassador who arrived on Hispaniola in 1590, was among the earliest Europeans to promote its use outside the continent. He brought its leaves to the court of Henry II, where it was ground into a fine powder and snorted. In the centuries that passed, it was largely chewed or smoked in pipes. On a thirty-acre farm in Raleigh, North Carolina, former Confederate soldiers who ended the war penniless began selling hand-rolled cigarettes to Union soldiers. The business, traveling through a few hands, would eventually become the

American Tobacco Company. In 1881 James Bonsack invented a cigarette-manufacturing machine, which was a complicated box that could roll 200 cigarettes a minute. The American Tobacco Company soon became the largest tobacco company in the world.

Half a century later, Americans discovered cigarettes had harmful health impacts. In 1949, a researcher working for the Medical Research Council named Richard Doll began studying lung cancer patients in London hospitals. In 649 cases of lung cancer, only two were non-smokers. Expanding the research only confirmed the results. In 1952, *Reader's Digest* published an article titled "Cancer by the Carton," and eight years later Luther Terry, the US Surgeon General, released a report that asserted smoking causes illness and death and urged action. What followed was a slow battle between public health advocates and the tobacco companies, which became notorious for funding their own studies minimizing the health impacts of tobacco, intended to sow doubt among consumers.

The official resolution to this small history came in 1998 with the Tobacco Master Settlement Agreement (MSA). Settling a number of class action lawsuits between the four largest US tobacco companies and the attorneys general of 46 states, the companies agreed to curtail or cease the marketing of their own products. Both the government and companies involved accepted that what was being sold was deadly with no positive side effects. On the boxes were health warnings telling customers not to buy them; in other countries, color images of skulls or diseased organs were printed on cartons to ensure the message would not be lost. In the decade after the agreement, cities and local municipalities began banning the use of cigarettes in closed social spaces, citing health concerns. With the introduction of a number of nicotine replacements—such as nicotine patches—meant to slowly wean those with nicotine addictions, it was understood that the habit of smoking would slowly cease to exist as knowledge of its dangers passed through the world's billions of people.

And yet, people still smoke. In 2008, a decade after the death knell of the tobacco industry was announced, the World

Health Organization named tobacco the world's single greatest preventable cause of death. People weren't quitting. In the midst of this, one of the many salves for former smokers exploded in popularity. The electronic cigarette, a strange invention originally designed and forgotten about in the mid-1960s, was suddenly being mass-produced in China beginning in 2003. These were small metal or plastic containers that stored an e-liquid, often a mixture that included various appealing flavors and nicotine in chemical form (though not all do). Many of them arrived on US soil via the internet, a commercial thoroughfare still too new to face significant regulation. An axiom of the last decade's cigarette debate was the understanding that smoke from the longstanding paper devices was toxic and that permitting it to freely blow in public space was tantamount to allowing walking smokestacks in public parks. The electronic cigarette—alternately known as the vape pen, vape pipes, or whatever website marketers thought would stick—evaded this public duty, as they did not emit the cancerous tar-tint of cigarettes, but rather a seemingly harmless watery vapor.

A decade passed and the purpose of these electronic devices remained foggy. Many contained no nicotine in them at all, creating a ghostly shadow of the smoking experience. Others lent themselves to entirely unrelated drug consumption, as substances like marijuana could also be reduced to a liquid and blown into vapor and leave almost none of its particular olfactory trace. Vapes could contain nothing and they could contain everything. They were fundamentally concealers, hiding chemicals safely inside an aroma that was so inoffensive it was easy to forget about the risks those chemicals carried with them, dousing the century of science in a new mystery.

At Issue: Vaping will attempt to parse that mystery. The story of the electronic cigarette, slipping out of the plastic of the dot com boom and emerging amid the lifestyle haze of brand names like Juul and Blu, is rich. It's proven not be a mere fad, and it may very well be our future.

Notes

1. "Defendant created an online culture and community targeted to young people and designed to encourage Juul use. Young people are flocking to this enticing and dangerous device," the suit alleged. "Juul Marketed to Minors, Hid Nicotine Levels, E-Cig User Says," *Law360*, October 11, 2018.

2. "The Price of Cool: A Teenager, a Juul and Nicotine Addiction," *The New York Times*, November 16, 2018.

3. "Notes from the Field: Use of Electronic Cigarettes and Any Tobacco Product Among Middle and High School Students," *CDC: Morbidity and Mortality Weekly Report*, November 16, 2018.

1

In Praise of Vaping: Better than Smoking

Jean-François Etter

Jean-François Etter is a professor of public health at the University of Geneva and is a longtime advocate of electronic cigarette usage.

The philosophy behind the design of electronic cigarettes was that they would bridge the divide between the moment in the late 1990s when cigarettes were collectively understood to be a public health menace and the future when they would not be smoked at all, making them a necessary evil. Jean-François Etter lays out the case that e-cigarettes must simply be safer than cigarettes to be useful.

Cigarette combustion, rather than either tobacco or nicotine, is the cause of a public health disaster. Fortunately, several new technologies that vaporize nicotine or tobacco, and may make cigarettes obsolete, have recently appeared. Research priorities include the effects of vaporizers on smoking cessation and initiation, their safety and toxicity, use by non-smokers, dual use of vaporizers and cigarettes, passive vaping, renormalization of smoking, and the development of messages that effectively communicate the continuum of risk for tobacco and nicotine products. A major difficulty is that we are chasing a moving target. New products constantly appear, and research results are often obsolete by the time they are published. Vaporizers do not need to be safe, only safer than cigarettes. However, harm reduction principles are often

"E-cigarettes: Methodological and Ideological Issues and Research Priorities," by Jean-François Etter, *BMC Medicine*, February 16, 2015. https://bmcmedicine.biomedcentral.com/articles/10.1186/s12916-014-0264-5. Licensed under CC BY 4.0 International.

misunderstood or rejected. In the context of a fierce ideological debate, and major investments by the tobacco industry, it is crucial that independent researchers provide regulators and the public with evidence-based guidance.

Background

The combustion of cigarettes, rather than either tobacco or nicotine, is the cause of a public health disaster. The cigarette-rolling machine, an innovation of the 19th century, bears much of the responsibility for this disaster. However, a series of 21st century innovations have the potential to revert the statistics back to the very low levels of tobacco-related mortality that existed before the advent of manufactured cigarettes, when tobacco was used mainly in non-combustible forms. Recent innovations include electronic cigarettes, vaporizers that heat tobacco but do not burn it, products similar to asthma inhalers that produce a nicotine aerosol, products that use a chemical reaction (pyruvate) to vaporize nicotine and products that use a flow of hot air to vaporize tobacco.[1-4] Given the profitability of this market, there is little doubt that other types of vaporizers will soon appear.

Scientists and regulators often react in a confused way to these disruptive technologies. The debate is highly ideological, and arguments are often misleading and even dishonest.[5] Negative reports on e-cigarettes tend to receive much media coverage, and, as a result, the proportion of smokers who think that e-cigarettes are more dangerous than combustible cigarettes is increasing.[6] In this context, it is crucial to provide regulators, clinicians, journalists and consumers with sound, evidence-based responses to their questions. However, there are hurdles on this path, both methodological and ideological.

Research Priorities

The impact of e-cigarettes and vaporizers on public health is the product of the damage caused or prevented by such products, multiplied by the number of people who adopt these products and stop using combustible cigarettes. From a regulatory point of view, the objective should be to minimize the harm to the population caused by all nicotine and tobacco products, including combustible cigarettes. Researchers should provide evidence to help regulators write reasonable regulations that take into account a continuum of risk for nicotine and tobacco products, are based on a principle of proportionality and do not stifle innovation. Research priorities include the effects of vaporizers on smoking cessation and initiation, safety and toxicity, use by non-smokers, dual use of vaporizers and cigarettes, use in public places (exposure to passive vaping and renormalization of smoking), flavors (toxicity and behavioral effects), nicotine (addictiveness, toxicity, risk perception) and the development of messages that effectively communicate the continuum of risk.

Methodological Issues

A major difficulty is that we are chasing a moving target. New products appear all the time, and research findings are often obsolete by the time they are published.

Most published studies on e-cigarettes are relatively short-term, but it is crucial to assess the long-term effects of these products on health and behavior. This will be costly and take years, and long-term studies will be outdated by the time they are published.

One important question is to assess whether e-cigarettes are a gateway to smoking or nicotine dependence in young non-smokers. We know from research on illicit drugs (Is cannabis a gateway to heroin?) that proving gateway effects requires methodologically sophisticated studies.[7] For e-cigarettes, all published studies to date that address gateway effects fall short of these methodological requirements.[4,8]

Assessing the effects of passive exposure to e-cigarette vapors is also politically relevant. However, given the very low levels of risk involved (probably orders of magnitude lower than for cigarette smoke), any health effect will be very hard to detect.

Ideological Bias

There is a continuum of risk for nicotine-containing products.[9,10] Harm reduction is about the lesser of two evils: vaporizers need to be safer than cigarettes, but not necessarily safe. Failure to admit this leads to negative attitudes towards reduced-risk products and to regulations that apply the same restrictions to all products. This is damaging to public health, as it hampers alternatives to combustible cigarettes. In many countries, nicotine vaporizers and smokeless tobacco cannot currently be advertised as reduced-risk products. Laws that prevent truthful communication about this continuum of risk prevent adoption of less harmful alternatives to combustible cigarettes.

The debate is loud but lacks robustness, and there is often an ideological bias against, and a lack of understanding of, harm reduction principles. There is also a willingness of the press and some scientists to emphasize the negative effects of e-cigarettes.[5] In particular, press releases issued by scientists or by their institutions sometimes do not reflect research findings.[11] This could be prevented by submitting press releases to the same peer-review process as that for scientific articles. The public has the right to an objective assessment of the situation, and to appropriate guidance, but at present this is not what it gets from many scientific articles, press reports and institutions.[5,11,12]

Conflicts of Interest

Most e-cigarette manufacturers have shown little interest in conducting or supporting peer-reviewed research. Much of the research is, therefore, conducted by independent researchers, but conflicts of interest are nevertheless present.[1] In contrast, research on other types of vaporizers (for example, heated tobacco products) is mainly conducted by the tobacco industry. For instance, Philip Morris International invested $2bn in research and development efforts for their four new vaporizing technologies.[13] To counterbalance this enormous investment, other funding sources (governments, foundations, crowdfunding) are needed to support independent researchers. A small tax (a few cents per unit) could be imposed on vaporizers to support independent research and education, but otherwise these products should be given a tax incentive.

The tobacco industry will probably soon dominate the nicotine/tobacco vaporizers market, not least because excessive regulation will make it too costly for smaller players to survive in a highly regulated environment. The tobacco industry will then be in a position to stifle this market, if it ends up being less profitable than tobacco cigarettes. Because of the dominant position of the tobacco industry, researchers and their institutions have little choice but to (reluctantly) reconsider their attitudes towards this industry. This is one of the thorniest issues in this field. The disclosure of conflicts of interest and registration of studies in open registries are necessary but insufficient first steps. An open debate, involving all stakeholders, is needed on this issue. Transparency and an appropriate approach to the management of conflicts of interest are necessary to preserve the integrity of research and public trust.

Conclusions

A window of opportunity is now open but will soon close. In the United States, the Food and Drug Administration is developing regulations that will apply to e-cigarettes and vaporizers, and European Union member states are now transposing the Tobacco Products Directive into national laws. Once these regulations are in place, they will be very difficult to change. However, because harm reduction strategies are often misunderstood or rejected,[14] there is a risk that e-cigarettes and vaporizers will be excessively regulated. Regulators must consider the unintended consequences of excessive regulation, and should be held accountable for any such consequences. Given that e-cigarettes and vaporizers are already much safer than combustible cigarettes, any benefit of regulations will be small, whereas the unintended consequences can have a large negative impact. Unfortunately, current proposals for regulation are often worse than the status quo. It is sad that this is happening with the help of some public health professionals, scientists and elected representatives of the people.

References

1. Pisinger C, Dossing M. A Systematic Review of Health Effects of Electronic Cigarettes. *Prev Med.* 2014;69C:248–60.

2. Weaver M, Breland A, Spindle T, Eissenberg T. Electronic Cigarettes: A Review of Safety and Clinical Issues. *J Addict Med.* 2014;8:234–40.

3. Rose JE, Turner JE, Murugesan T, Behm FM, Laugesen M. Pulmonary Delivery of Nicotine Pyruvate: Sensory and Pharmacokinetic Characteristics. *Exp Clin Psychopharmacol.* 2010;18:385–94.

4. Hajek P, Etter JF, Benowitz N, Eissenberg T, McRobbie H. Electronic Cigarettes: Review of Use, Content, Safety, Effects on Smokers and Potential for Harm and Benefits. *Addiction.* 2014;109:1801–10.

5. McNeill A, Etter JF, Farsalinos K, Hajek P, le Houezec J, McRobbie H. A Critique of a World Health Organization-Commissioned Report and Associated Paper on Electronic Cigarettes. *Addiction.* 2014;109:2128–34.

6. Tan AS, Bigman CA. E-Cigarette Awareness and Perceived Harmfulness: Prevalence and Associations with Smoking-Cessation Outcomes. *Am J Prev Med.* 2014;47:141–9.

7. Kandel DB, Yamaguchi K, Klein LC. Testing the Gateway Hypothesis. *Addiction.* 2006;101:470–2. discussion 474–6.

8. Pepper JK, Brewer NT. Electronic Nicotine Delivery System (Electronic Cigarette) Awareness, Use, Reactions and Beliefs: A Systematic Review. *Tob Control.* 2014; 23:375–84.

9. Nutt DJ, Phillips LD, Balfour D, Curran HV, Dockrell M, Foulds J, et al. Estimating the Harms of Nicotine-Containing Products Using the MCDA Approach. *Eur Addict Res.* 2014;20:218–25.

10. Zeller M, Hatsukami D, Strategic Dialogue on Tobacco Harm Reduction Group. The Strategic Dialogue on Tobacco Harm Reduction: A Vision and Blueprint for Action in the US. *Tob Control.* 2009;18:324–32.

11. Lerner K. E-Cigarette Group Calls CDC Study on Teen Use Deceptive. *Law360.* http://www.law360.com/articles/572188/e-cigarette-group-calls-cdc-study-on-teen-use-deceptive. Accessed 4 Dec 2014.

12. West R. Electronic Cigarettes: Getting the Science Right and Communicating It Accurately. *Addiction.* 2014. Online first. http://onlinelibrary.wiley.com/journal/10.1111/%28ISSN%291360-0443/homepage/electronic_cigarettes.htm.

13. Mulier T, Thesing G. Philip Morris Sees $700 Million Boost From iQOS Smoking Device. *Bloomberg.* http://www.bloomberg.com/news/2014-06-26/philip-morris-sees-700-million-boost-from-iqos-smoking-device.html. Accessed Jan 12, 2015.

14. Kozlowski LT. Ending versus Controlling versus Employing Addiction in the Tobacco-Caused Disease Endgame: Moral Psychological Perspectives. *Tob Control.* 2013; 22:i31–2.

2

The Case for Regulation

Eric A. Feldman

Eric A. Feldman is a professor of law and medical ethics & health policy at the University of Pennsylvania Law School. His books and articles generally explore the comparative dimensions of rights, dispute resolution, and legal culture in the context of urgent policy issues.

In this viewpoint, Eric A. Feldman discusses how e-cigarettes can be situated inside current regulatory framework and covers the relatively brief history of its regulation. While e-cigarettes were initially sold freely as a curiosity, they quickly became a sensation that promised the reemergence of smoking. At first the FDA sought to call them drugs and drug delivery devices, categorizing them as anti-smoking medication, but savvy marketing on the part of leading manufacturers, some of whom were quietly taken over by old tobacco multinationals, eluded this approach.

Just a few years ago, it was impossible to imagine that e-cigarettes would become a popular consumer product. They seemed so gimmicky, so obviously unsatisfying, so fake, so un-cool; who could conceivably be attracted to the idea of sucking on a piece of plastic, inhaling an addictive substance, and exhaling an ephemeral

Eric A. Feldman, "Layers of Law: The Case of E-Cigarettes," 10 FIU L. Rev. 111 (2014). Available at: h3p://ecollections.law.2u.edu/lawreview/vol10/iss1/10. This Article is brought to you for free and open access by eCollections @ FIU Law Library. It has been accepted for inclusion in FIU Law Review by an authorized administrator of eCollections @ FIU Law Library.

vapor? Even worse, e-cigarettes lacked certain qualities that made conventional cigarettes so popular, like the ritual of lighting up, the smell of smoke, and the aesthetic of a smoke-filled room, but had the drawback of containing addictive quantities of nicotine. From almost every perspective, e-cigarettes seemed unlikely to gain traction in the marketplace.

The expectation—for some a hope—that e-cigarettes had little market potential was also propelled by the tobacco control community's sense that it was finally winning what had come to be called the "tobacco wars." *Tobacco Control*, for example, a journal published by the prestigious *British Medical Journal*, titled its May 2013 issue "The Tobacco Endgame." Authors in that issue announced that the final days of smoking had arrived, noting that cigarette consumption was declining throughout the developed world and that multinational tobacco companies were on the defensive. Similarly, the fiftieth anniversary of the US Surgeon General's 1964 *Report on Tobacco and Health* represented a milestone in the tobacco control effort and made the second decade of the new millennium an opportune time to celebrate the triumph of public health over the preventable harms caused by smoking.

The celebration, however, was premature. With rapidity and stealth, the appearance of e-cigarettes threatened the idea that smoking was a dying habit. Borrowing the shape and size of cigarettes but utilizing twenty-first-century vaporizing technology, the new e-cigarette devices raised the possibility that the decline of tobacco-related morbidity and mortality would be stalled by a product that was evocative of conventional cigarettes and might entice a new generation of smokers. Moreover, in the eyes of many in the tobacco control community, the acceptance of e-cigarettes challenged one of the central strategic priorities of tobacco control—the "denormalization" of smoking. Successfully doing so had the potential to lead to a resurgence of smoking.

[...]

Moreover, the absence of shared social norms about the product (e- cigarettes) and behavior (vaping, i.e., using e-cigarettes) further invites a multiplicity of e-cigarette regulations. If there were data demonstrating that e-cigarettes caused health harms to users or bystanders, it would surely influence the informal rules of conduct that developed to govern their use. In the absence of such widely-accepted data, however, the health impact of vaping does not serve as a constraint on the types of vaping norms that are seen as appropriate. In short, the lack of widespread scientific agreement about the health impact of vaping, along with the absence of shared social norms about vaping, are at least in part responsible for the divergent types of e-cigarette regulations promoted by international bodies, local and national government, industry, and small private enterprises.

[...]

Challenges to the Regulation of E-Cigarettes

At least initially, the rise of e-cigarettes occurred in a legal vacuum. Even as it became clear that at least some sort of legal response was necessary—there was near-consensus, for example, that sales to children should be prohibited—the nature of the response remained uncertain. There was little agreement about whether e-cigarette regulation should be local, national or transnational; punitive or permissive; or whether it should utilize the framework of tobacco regulation, pharmaceutical regulation, or consumer protection.

One initial challenge was that regulators had to be able to describe the product they were regulating. Automobile safety regulations, for example, depend upon a definition of an automobile that distinguishes it from a truck, a motorcycle, and a bicycle. But there is no set definition of an "e-cigarette." The technical terms for e-cigarettes, "non-combustible tobacco products" and "electronic nicotine delivery systems," do not do an adequate job of describing the wide array of products that have entered (and continue to enter) the market as e-hookahs, hookah pens, hookah sticks, vape pens, vape pipes, and more. Those who use these devices sometimes (but rarely) call themselves smokers, instead preferring the term "vaper," as in "those who use products that produce vapor rather than smoke." The products come in a dizzying array of shapes, colors, and styles, make use of different technologies, and are rapidly evolving. As a result, it is difficult to define the class of products subject to regulation, and consequently to issue regulations with the desired scope.

Uncertainty about the health impact of e-cigarettes was (and continues to be) a significant impediment to regulation. Evidence that e-cigarettes are harmful to the health of vapers, or that vaping imposes harms on bystanders, may invite certain types of regulation, such as age restrictions, bans on use in certain settings, taxation, and perhaps more. Similarly, evidence that the use of e-cigarettes serves as a gateway to smoking suggests a different regulatory posture than evidence that the use of e-cigarettes facilitates smoking cessation. Unfortunately, not enough is yet known about the health impact of e-cigarettes or their effect on smoking-related behavior. The FDA has this to say:

> *E-cigarettes have not been fully studied, so consumers currently don't know the potential risks of e-cigarettes when used as intended, how much nicotine or other potentially harmful chemicals are being inhaled during use, or whether there are any benefits associated with using these products. Additionally, it is not known whether e-cigarettes may lead young people to try other tobacco products, including conventional cigarettes, which are known to cause disease and lead to premature death.*

[...]

Underlying such scientific assessments is the fact that e-cigarettes, like combustible tobacco products, contain nicotine. The oft-repeated statement that "smokers smoke for the nicotine but die from the tar" is a useful reminder that nicotine is not what makes conventional cigarettes so harmful. Instead, the carcinogens contained in tobacco leaf, which are not found in e-cigarettes, are what lead to tobacco-related disease. [David B.] Abrams' view that e-cigarettes are likely to be significantly less harmful than tobacco cigarettes is therefore plausible, though it does not account for the possibility that using e-cigarettes could potentially serve as a gateway to smoking, that dual use (of combustible and electronic cigarettes) may become common, and that much remains unknown about chemical-containing vapor.

The sparseness of data on the public health impact of e-cigarettes has invited a volatile conflict between those in the US public health community pressing for a precautionary approach to e-cigarettes and others insisting on a harm reduction strategy. From the precautionary perspective, uncertainty about the potential public health harms of e-cigarettes demands regulatory action. As Thomas Frieden, Director of the Centers for Disease Control and Prevention (CDC) puts it, "I think the precautionary principle—better safe than sorry—rules here." In contrast, prioritizing harm reduction suggests a less aggressive regulatory posture that underscores the likelihood that e-cigarettes are less hazardous than combustible cigarettes and have the potential to improve public health by reducing per capita cigarette consumption. Those who subscribe to a harm reduction perspective believe that embracing the precautionary principle could mute the potential of e-cigarettes to reduce tobacco-related morbidity and mortality.

Despite their differences, most public health experts agree that e-cigarettes need at least some regulation. Their popularity has exploded in the past five years, as evidenced by the opening of over 16,000 vape shops in the US, a dramatic increase in the sale of e-cigarette products, and a rapid rise in the number of people trying e-cigarettes. The fastest growing segment of the market is vaporizers, often called e-hookahs or vape pens, which lack the shape and color of traditional tobacco cigarettes, have larger batteries than most e-cigarettes, and contain large refillable chambers that hold e-juice, the nicotine-containing liquid that is vaporized by e-cigarettes. Users of such products can purchase e-juice in bulk both at specialty stores and online, with different flavorings and a range of nicotine concentrations. Because e-juice is unregulated, there is the potential for significant and potentially dangerous variation in how much nicotine particular products contains, and in the safety of other ingredients contained in those products. One relatively uncontroversial step in regulating e-cigarettes, therefore, would be to set standards for the safety and quality of the increasingly popular refillable liquids used by vapers.

In addition to product standards, some public health experts and regulators see the need for a significantly more robust set of regulations to combat the rapid changes that have occurred in the e-cigarette industry. In the early days of e-cigarettes, 2007-2011, hundreds of companies in the US imported e-cigarette products from China, competing in a small but rapidly evolving market. As e-cigarettes grew in popularity, those companies were pushed aside by multinational tobacco companies, which are now the key players in the e-cigarette market. Lorillard, for example, purchased the market-leading e-cigarette in the US, Blu, for $135 million in 2012 and sold it in 2014 (along with several of its tobacco brands) to Imperial Tobacco in a multi-billion dollar deal. Altria introduced MarkTen during the summer of 2014, Philip Morris International (PMI), began test marketing IQOS (the result of ten years and two billion dollars in R&D) in Italy and Japan in late 2014, and in that same year purchased a UK e-cigarette company, Nicocigs. PMI officials are enthusiastic about the future of e-cigarettes, pronouncing such products "our greatest growth opportunity in the years to come, which we believe has the very real potential to transform the industry." Other major tobacco companies have not been left behind: R.J. Reynolds released Vuse in 2014; Japan Tobacco International (JTI) owns a minority interest in Ploom; and British American Tobacco owns Vype. Indeed all of the major tobacco industry players have rapidly embraced the e-cigarette business.

For those who have long labored to improve public health by reducing tobacco-related morbidity and mortality, the reappearance of their traditional foe—"big tobacco"—is an unwelcome surprise. Douglas Bettcher, Director of the World Health Organization's Department for the Prevention of Noncommunicable Diseases, makes the case in blunt terms: "[t]he tobacco industry has a history of deception when using harm-reduction marketing ploys to promote tobacco products with the pretense of being less harmful." Similarly, three prominent tobacco control researchers have noted how the traditional tobacco companies are "using the same political and public relations strategies" that were deployed to market combustible tobacco. In their view, the tobacco companies are likely to hide the potential dangers of e-cigarettes while aggressively and effectively marketing them. Indeed, their marketing prowess is already evident. Because the legal prohibitions on most tobacco advertising and sponsorship do not apply to e-cigarettes, one can already see a steady increase in spending on e-cigarette advertising. Ads promoting e-cigarettes are found in a wide range of magazines; racing cars are covered in e-cigarette designs; cartoon characters are used for product promotion; ads have even found their way into that most hallowed of television advertising slots, the Super Bowl. Like their tobacco predecessors, e-cigarette ads feature rugged men and attractive women, often famous actors and actresses, stress freedom and independence, promote the "sexiness" of vaping, and underscore the contrast between the negative association of smoking tobacco cigarettes and the positives of using e-cigarettes. The rapid increase in the use of e-cigarettes may in significant part be a result of those advertising dollars.

E-cigarette companies, in addition to conventional marketing efforts, have also engaged in a battle over the social acceptance and meaning of vaping. Public health advocates had for years worked to counter the tobacco industry's valorization of smoking by promoting the view that smoking was an unappealing, anti-social, smelly habit and that smokers were deviant and foolish. The marketers of e-cigarettes picked up on that argument and promoted e-cigarettes as a route to the "renormalization" of cigarette-like products. They have highlighted the difference between combustible and non-combustible products, insisting that the demonization of smokers and smoking should not be carried over to vapers and vaping. The industry's explicit engagement of the denormalization of smoking is well illustrated by Lorillard's "take back your freedom" advertising campaign for Blu e-cigarettes, which promotes vaping as an opportunity for smokers to regain the moral high-ground by using a product that warrants social acceptance.

So far, those efforts have met with only limited success. Although e-cigarettes are not yet tarnished by the powerfully negative view of combustible tobacco products, social norms about vaping are still evolving. Neither those who use e-cigarettes, nor the population more generally, have yet determined the content of the informal social rules governing vaping, such as whether it is acceptable to use e-cigarettes in restaurants, in public parks, or around kids. Unwritten rules of social conduct are also lacking when it comes to e-cigarette use in homes, workplaces, social settings, cinemas, stadiums, beaches, or at sporting events, and the jury is out when it comes to the question of whether vaping is cool or ridiculous, sexy or silly, macho or emasculating.

There is nothing subtle about the battle for social acceptability. Soon after a former smoker who turned to vaping published an article in *Business Insider* titled "The 9 Laws of E-Cigarettiquette: A Handy Guide for Smokers," various e-cigarette companies reprinted his "laws" and invited a discussion among vapers about what constitutes appropriate vaping conduct. Among the "laws" of "e-cigarettiquette" proposed in the article are:

- Puffing on your e-cigarette at the movies is not allowed;
- Do not vape at the dinner table;
- Don't vape in the bathroom;
- Cigarette smokers are not your inferiors, don't act like it;
- Don't leave a trail of e-cig wrappers and cartridges lying around.

Although the specific issues are trivial the general point is not. Public health researchers appreciate that the battle over the social acceptability of vaping is at the heart of the e-cigarette debate, and cite the battle over "renormalization" as the central issue in the regulation of e-cigarettes.

[...]

The Web of E-Cigarette Regulations
[...]

Japan

Japan's approach to e-cigarettes is shaped by the history of the government's tobacco monopoly, particularly the fact that the Ministry of Finance has the legal authority to regulate tobacco products and continues to be a controlling shareholder in Japan's only domestic tobacco company, Japan Tobacco. Tax revenues from tobacco sales have long defined the government's regulatory objective in the tobacco area, and political support by the agricultural sector (within which tobacco farmers have been influential) has further muted the state's interest in regulations that might decrease domestic tobacco consumption. The interesting regulatory question raised by e-cigarettes in Japan is whether they are tobacco products subject to control by the Ministry of Finance (MoF), or if they fall under the Ministry of Health, Labor, and Welfare's (MHLW) authority over pharmaceutical products.

[...]

United States

The situation in the US has certain similarities to that in Japan. In both countries, e-cigarette companies would prefer to be regulated under the relatively lenient standards that govern tobacco products, rather than under the laws governing pharmaceutical products, which involve time consuming and expensive data collection with no guarantee of product approval. Whereas Japanese regulators concluded that e-cigarettes containing nicotine were pharmaceutical products subject to MHLW control, however, the US Food and Drug Administration's (FDA) effort to assert regulatory authority over e-cigarettes as combination drugs/delivery devices met with less success.

In October 2008, the FDA detained a number of shipments of electronic cigarettes at the Los Angeles International Airport. The e-cigarettes were being imported from China by two e-cigarette companies, NJOY and Smoking Everywhere, but the FDA claimed that importing these nicotine-containing products violated the Food, Drug, and Cosmetic Act (FDCA) because they had not yet been evaluated by the FDA for safety and efficacy, as required for all drugs marketed in the US. The FDA therefore ordered the companies to either export or destroy the e-cigarettes within ninety days. During the ensuing fourteen months the FDA refused entry to dozens of additional shipments of e-cigarettes. According to FDA Commissioner Margaret Hamburg, "[t]he FDA is concerned about the safety of these products and how they are marketed to the public."

E-cigarette importers, not surprisingly, had a different view. By carefully avoiding claims about the therapeutic effects of e-cigarettes—as a treatment for nicotine withdrawal, for example—they argued that their products did not fall within the FDA's jurisdiction over drugs and drug delivery devices. Instead, if the FDA was going to regulate e-cigarettes, importers argued that it could only do so under its recently acquired power to regulate tobacco products. They demanded that the FDA put a halt to the detention of their products, and brought their claim to the DC Circuit Court.

In a stinging rebuke to the FDA's position, later affirmed on appeal, US District Court Judge Richard Leon ruled that the FDA could not regulate e-cigarettes as drugs or drug delivery devices unless the products were marketed with claims about their therapeutic effects. Judge Leon did not simply disagree with the FDA; he scolded the agency in the harshest of tones:

> *This case appears to be yet another example of FDA's aggressive efforts to regulate recreational tobacco products as drugs or devices under the Food, Drug, and Cosmetic Act (FDCA). Ironically, notwithstanding that Congress has now taken the unprecedented step of granting FDA jurisdiction over those products, FDA remains undeterred. Unfortunately, its tenacious drive to maximize its regulatory power has resulted in its advocacy of an interpretation of the relevant law that I find, at first blush, to be unreasonable and unacceptable.*

In April 2014, more than four years later, the FDA announced its intention to extend its regulatory authority over tobacco to e-cigarettes and a variety of other "tobacco products" like cigars and hookah.

[...]

Conclusion

Law and society scholars have long appreciated that law exists in "many rooms." Rare is the situation in which a simple legal text is all that it takes to create or control behavior. If it were, speed limits would have put an end to speeding, and copyright laws would have ended illegal music downloads. Instead, social control—the effort to create and maintain social order by the state and private parties—depends upon a complex brew of coercion and persuasion, hard laws and soft nudges, far-reaching pronouncements and narrowly tailored rules.

E-cigarettes provide an opportunity to examine the early stages of a wide-ranging effort to impose a set of legal controls on a new product that is enjoying a rapid increase in popularity. In some ways, it is a simple and predictable story. Uncertainty about a new product results in uncertainty about whether and how it should be regulated, which regulatory body is responsible for creating whatever regulations are deemed necessary, and how to ensure that the regulations have the desired effect. Although uncertainty is almost always a feature of policymaking, especially in the area of public health, the rapid innovation of e-cigarette technology, along with the fast uptick in the popularity of vaping, have created a greater degree of uncertainty than usual. The result has been the emergence of a complex web of e-cigarette-related legal rules and social norms.

3

The Origins of Nicotine Regulation

Shital A. Patel

Shital Patel was on the staff of the DePaul Journal of Health Care Law.

If e-cigarettes are viewed as simply the latest stage in the history of smoke, looking at key events in the history of tobacco regulation can help contextualize current regulatory attempts. Shital A. Patel's 2005 report extends from a time when "approximately 80% of adult smokers started smoking before the age of 18" to today, when smoking indoors is often forbidden. A lot of these changes can be attributed to the 1998 Master Settlement Agreement between the country's largest cigarette manufacturers and the legal teams of 46 states. In addition to mandating payments from tobacco companies, it also limited the ways tobacco could be marketed and aided in defining both what a tobacco product is and where it could be bought, sold, or smoked.

> *"What is different about tobacco litigation, however, is that the potential claimants are so numerous, the scope of the offending conduct so vast and the resources of the defendants so huge, that conventional litigation is simply inadequate to capture and contain the issues or assure appropriate relief. It thus fails as both a policy and a compensatory vehicle."*
>
> *-Arthur B. LaFrance, Tobacco Litigation: Smoke, Mirrors, and Public Policy, 26 AM. J.L. & MED. 187, 189 (2000).*

Shital A. Patel, "The Tobacco Litigation Merry-Go-Round: Did the MSA Make It Stop?" DePaul J. Health Care L. 615 (2005). Available at: https://via.library.depaul.edu/jhcl/vol8/iss3/4. This Article is brought to you for free and open access by the College of Law at Via Sapientiae. It has been accepted for inclusion in DePaul Journal of Health Care Law by an authorized editor of Via Sapientiae.

Background: Smoking As a Health Issue

While the problem of smoking and tobacco-related illnesses may have already fatigued the ears of the public health, the problem bears at least brief consideration in light of what led to such a colossal deal as the Master Settlement Agreement. Why such a public outcry against the tobacco industry? Why smoking? The subject of tobacco control, much like gun control and abortion, sparks heated debate. Opinions span the gamut from fiercely protective of the right to use tobacco freely to staunch advocates of government regulation or abolition of cigarettes because of second-hand smoke danger. The stakes of smoking, nonetheless, are vast. Tobacco kills more Americans than AIDS, drugs, homicides, fires, and automobile accidents combined. Globally, smoking-related deaths will rise to 10 million per year by 2030 and 7 million of these deaths will occur in less than industrialized nations. Worldwide, tobacco products kill approximately 4.9 million people per year.

Irrespective of whether tobacco companies continue to advertise to young people, smoking is clearly a significant problem among youth. Approximately 80% of adult smokers started smoking before the age of 18. Every day, nearly five thousand young people under the age of 18 try their first cigarette. Two thousand of them will then become daily smokers. If the current smoking patterns in the United States persist, an estimated 6.4 million of today's children will die prematurely of tobacco-related diseases. During the decade prior to the MSA, youth smoking was on the rise, according to the National Cancer Institute, and approximately 35% of youth were smokers in 1999. According to a June 2001 report released by the Federal Interagency Forum on Child and Family Statistics, adolescent cigarette use is declining. This report indicates that smoking by eighth, tenth, and twelfth grade students peaked just before the MSA and has decreased since then.

Smoking is not a cost-free vice to American taxpayers. Direct medical expenditures attributed to smoking amount to more than $75 billion per year in the United States. Furthermore, smoking costs an estimated $80 billion per year in lost productivity. Each of the approximately 22 billion packs of cigarettes sold in the US in 1999 cost the nation an estimated $7.18 in medical care costs and lost productivity.

The US Department of Health and Human Services asserts that tobacco control saves money. For example, an economic assessment found that a health care plan's annual cost of covering treatment to help people quit smoking ranged from $0.89 to $4.92 per smoker, whereas the annual cost of treating smoking-related illness ranged from $6.00 to $33.00 per smoker. Recent studies have concluded that reducing smoking prevalence among pregnant women by one percentage point over 7 years would prevent 57,200 low-birth weight births and save $572 million.

What does the current smoking problem look like? According to a study released in October 2003 by the Centers for Disease Control and Prevention (CDC), the percentage of American adults who regularly smoke cigarettes fell slightly in 2001. The CDC welcomed these findings, attributing them in part to state anti-tobacco programs funded by the tobacco companies pursuant to the Master Settlement Agreement. However, Dr. Corinne Husten, medical officer in the CDC's Office of Smoking and Health warned, "The states were starting to fund some comprehensive tobacco-prevention and control programs, but unfortunately with the budget crisis those funds are being lost and put into general revenues." Most states are, in fact, failing to use their portion of the multi-billion dollar settlement dollars from the tobacco industry to fund tobacco prevention and cessation efforts.

History of the Master Settlement Agreement

In order to create an analytical framework for the tobacco litigation that followed the MSA, it is useful to develop a very brief overview of the events leading up to the settlement. Before the early 1950s, the tobacco industry's image remained unaffected by litigation and negative media attention to their products. This all changed with the publication of a *Reader's Digest* article entitled, "Cancer by the Carton" in 1952. Two years later, the tobacco industry faced its first lawsuit. Eva Cooper, whose husband died of lung cancer, sued R.J. Reynolds. This was the first liability suit by a lung cancer victim alleging negligence and breach of warranty. Cooper lost the suit because the court ruled that there was no evidence that smoking caused cancer. The tobacco industry managed to outspend and outlast plaintiffs for years. From 1954 to 1994, approximately 813 claims were filed by private citizens in tort actions in state courts against tobacco companies. Only twice did the courts find [in] favor of the plaintiffs, and both decisions were subsequently reversed on appeal.

It was Diane Castano's 1994 case, nonetheless, that grew into the nation's largest class action suit of smokers. In 1996, the court struck down the class action status of the Castano case, calling it too unwieldy to cover all states.

"No court has ever tried an injury-as-addiction case … The Castano class suffers from many of the difficulties that the Georgine court found dispositive. The class members were exposed to nicotine through different products, for different amounts of time, and over different time periods. Each class member's knowledge about the effects of smoking differs, and each plaintiff began smoking for different reasons. Each of these factual differences impacts the application of legal rules such as causation, reliance, comparative fault, and other affirmative defenses."

The tobacco industry became a public health pariah as an onslaught of individual liability suits occurred and as the federal government began to investigate the industry's actions. Each of the seven executives of the leading tobacco manufacturers, including Philip Morris, R.J. Reynolds, Lorillard, and Brown & Williamson, testified and swore during the Waxman Congressional hearings that they "believe nicotine is not addictive." At the same time, the states' legal crusade against the tobacco industry began taking hold, on both the litigation and legislative fronts. Mississippi Attorney General Mike Moore filed the first state lawsuit against the industry in May 1994, explaining that the case was "premised on a simple notion—you cause the health crisis, you pay for it."

Upon the gathering momentum among the states, the industry signaled a willingness to discuss settlement in early 1997. During the congressional deliberations, however, the tobacco companies had negotiated individual settlements with four states that had advanced farthest down the litigation trail—Florida, Minnesota, Texas and Mississippi. After the national settlement proposal settlement failed in Congress, the state and tobacco companies returned to the bargaining table. On November 16, 1998 a "Master Settlement Agreement" was announced between the four largest tobacco companies—known as the "Majors"—and the remaining forty-six states, the District of Columbia, and five US Territories, collectively referred to in this article as "the states."

Each state action lists two primary goals and forms of relief: first, to recover state funds expended in treating tobacco-related illness through its Medicaid or state employee health insurance plan and second, to enjoin the tobacco companies from engaging in any marketing that may appeal to underage consumers of tobacco products. "During a press conference following the release of the MSA, Washington Attorney General Christine Gregoire stated that these two aims were critical to the success of the settlement negotiations. The MSA directly states these goals in the agreement that representatives of the settling states signed the agreement "in order … to reduce youth smoking, to promote public health and to secure monetary payments" to the states.

The monetary sum agreed to in the MSA required the tobacco companies to pay $10 billion per year to the states over the course of twenty-five years, until the year 2023. In addition, the tobacco companies agreed to "contribute" $1.5 billion over five years to an anti-smoking education and advertising campaign and $250 million to a foundation dedicated to reducing teen smoking. The net present value of these payments to the states pursuant to the MSA has been estimated at $281.6 billion.

[…]

Why Did They Settle?

[...]

One of the practical theories of why the tobacco companies would agree to make such lavish payments to the states and live under new regulatory constraints is to gain protection from bankruptcy and loss of market share. The financial stakes in the state suits were great because the tobacco manufacturers faced a line of state plaintiffs, who could learn from one another's trials, and slowly drain the defendant's finances. Another perspective proposes that the tobacco industry benefits because the MSA cartelizes industry and guards against destabilization of the cartel by erecting barriers to entry that preserve the 99 percent market dominance of the tobacco giants.

[...]

Provisions Affecting the Marketing of Tobacco Products

A major consequence of the Master Settlement Agreement is the severe limitations imposed on the marketing, advertising, and promotion of tobacco and tobacco products. The advertising restrictions are a complex thicket of legalese and cross-references among definitions. In order to gain a basic understanding of the kinds of advertising limitations imposed by the MSA, this article will present a simplified overview of the advertising restrictions, which are very specifically defined in the MSA itself.

The MSA bans "outdoor advertising," which includes billboards, and signs in arenas, video arcades, stadia, and shopping malls. Specific types of outdoor advertising are banned, as well as certain advertisements placed inside a store if they are still visible from the outside. However, a significant exception to these "outdoor advertising" bans is that they do not apply to tobacco retail locations, the places most interested in displaying tobacco advertising." A tobacco retailer may place an unlimited number of tobacco advertisements and promotions anywhere on that property as long as the displays are smaller than fourteen square feet. It has been criticized that this exception for tobacco retailers substantially undercuts the "outdoor advertising" bans. Thus, a gas station selling cigarettes must abide by the "outdoor advertising" bans, but a tobacco shop does not.

[...]

Consistent with the provision to cease targeting youth, the MSA bans the use of cartoon images in the advertising, promotion, packaging, or labeling of tobacco products. Incorporated within this ban of cartoon images are depictions of objects, people, or animal creatures with comically exaggerated features or superhuman powers.

4

The History of Smoking

Jason Hughes

Jason Hughes is head of the department of media, communication, and sociology at the University of Leicester in the United Kingdom. His recent research has focused extensively on e-cigarette usage among young people.

Most writing about electronic cigarettes begins already situated in a world where a number of people commit the public and personal health hazard of smoking, treating it as something that must be negotiated with. Jason Hughes provides the long view of tobacco smoking, situating the use of electronic cigarettes into the longer history of smoking tobacco and the early advent of "smokeless smoking," a kind of cigarette that precedes electronic cigarettes but seems to anticipate their arrival.

My overriding question for this paper is a classic process sociological one: *How did this come to be?* More specifically, how and why have e-cigarettes become increasingly popular? More fundamentally, I am interested in the question of how tobacco came to be consumed as, essentially, a nicotine solution that is "vaped." How, to put it provocatively, did smoke come to be erased from smoking?

My core argument is that in order to understand the ascendancy of e-cigarettes it is necessary to have a look at the long history of tobacco use in order to make sense of present-day practices. This is consistent with a sociological position which draws much from the work of Norbert Elias: that social reality can only be properly apprehended as a set of long-term processes, and as such, we should avoid a "retreat to the present" without any sense of how this came to be.

Following from this position, my starting point is that tobacco use—what tobacco is understood and employed to do to and for the people who consume it—fundamentally shifts over time. By this I mean that material tobacco (the plant, how it is cultivated, cured, processed, and otherwise modified); the primary mode of its consumption (e.g. whether it is smoked or chewed); the practices and understandings surrounding its use (the rituals, the applications, the cultural associations); its purposes (the functions it is understood to perform for a user); and how its effects are experienced by users (the feelings generated by its consumption and how these are perceived), must all be understood as long-term processes, not fixed "categories" that we can take as "given." Thus, significantly, while it is now common to use the term smoking to refer to the consumption of tobacco, it is noteworthy that a number of substances—phencyclidine (PCP), methamphetamine, crack cocaine, opium, cannabis, etc.—have characteristically been smoked as the primary mode of their consumption. Conversely, over the last few millennia, tobacco has been licked, blown, ocularly absorbed, drunk (tobacco juice), ingested, snuffed, topically applied, and anally injected, to name but a few of the ways it has been used.

So where might we begin to look at this long-term set of developments? The plant was introduced into Europe in mid-to-late 1500s by explorers of the "new world." But tobacco was used for thousands of years by Amerindian peoples prior to contact with Europeans. It makes sense then, to "begin" our process there. As a way of helping structure this "broad" brush account of the development of tobacco, I've divided up the historical material into three phases: pre-modern, early-modern, and modern tobacco use.

It should be noted, of course, that real world processes rarely can be so neatly delineated into "stages" or "phases" in this manner. The divide thus serves heuristic more than ontological purposes.

Pre-Modern Use

Metsé inhaled deeply, and as he finished one cigarette an attending shaman handed him another lighted one. Metsé inhaled all the smoke, and soon began to evince considerable physical distress. After about ten minutes his right leg began to tremble. Later his left arm began to twitch. He swallowed smoke as well as inhaling it, and soon was groaning in pain ... He took another cigarette and continued to inhale until he was near to collapse ... Suddenly he "died," flinging his arms outward and straightening his legs stiffly ... He remained in this state of collapse nearly fifteen minutes ... (Dole 1964: 57-8).

The above extract describes the usage of tobacco by a tobacco shaman. While the account was collected in the twentieth century, the ritual described involves practices that date back to pre-Columbian times in the Americas. Pre-Columbian Amerindian tobacco use typically involved the consumption of strains and varieties of tobacco that were much stronger than those of latter day cigarettes. Tobacco was, more than any other psychoactive substance, used extensively in shamanistic ritual. There is a wealth of documented evidence to suggest that the tobacco used in the "old world" was fully capable of inducing hallucinations, including many early (bewildered) colonial accounts of "*godlesse*" natives using the substance to fall into "death-like" trances. A key component of much Amerindian cosmology holds that only through overcoming "death" that one is able to "treat" it. Understandings and practices surrounding tobacco and its use varied widely, but a common theme was that tobacco was a sacred plant that hinged together the physical and spiritual world. Tobacco-induced intoxication was thus a means of "communing with the spirits"; and the plant plus ascending tobacco smoke had enormous symbolic potency. Shamanistic "deaths" could last up to fifteen minutes, and would sometimes lead to actual deaths from acute nicotine intoxication. The evidence from ethnopharmacological research suggests that the chief pharmacological agent in the tobacco consumed was nicotine, though other psychoactive alkaloids present in rustic strains of tobacco might also have had a role to play, particularly when combined with high doses of nicotine. In fact, anthropological accounts suggest that the tobacco plant was used more than any other in Amerindian shamanistic ritual, principally because its effects were predictable and relatively short-lived. Recreational use of tobacco among "old world" Amerindians—and it is problematic to make any simple blanket generalisations—was typically less dramatic, but still involved relatively potent strains that would in many cases be smoked sitting down, often inducing intoxication and unconsciousness (see, for a fuller account of Native American tobacco use, Wilbert 1987).

Early-Modern Use

Tobacco was first brought to the Court and gardens of the European aristocracy and secular upper classes in sixteenth century by returning travellers from the Americas. It was quickly hailed to be a "panacea": a cure-all that was prescribed as a remedy for an impressive array of ailments—everything from toothache to cancer. Part of the reason for tobacco's success was that it fitted well with the system of medical cosmology that was prevalent in early-modern Europe. Briefly, the prevailing understandings by leading physicians held that the body was made up of different "humours" such as blood, bile, and phlegm. These humours had different properties—they could be hot or cold, dry or moist. If someone was phlegmatic, they had a surplus of mucous (typically, a cold, moist humour)—and were typically dispassionate and emotionally "cold." Conversely, if someone was "sanguine," they were likely "hot blooded"—evident, for example, in their ruddy complexion and an optimistic disposition. It is noteworthy that there was no simple divide between ailments of the mind and body, all were seen to be part of the same malaise. The goal of humoural medicine, then, was to restore bodily equilibrium. Too much hot bloodedness could be corrected by bloodletting, particularly through the application of leeches. Similarly, an excess of cold, moist humours (we still talk about having a "cold" today) could be corrected by ingesting a substance that was "hot and dry." Tobacco was understood as one such substance that was particularly well suited to "dissipating evil humours" on account of it being "hot and dry in the second order." The evidence for tobacco's efficacy was confirmed by the spitting, coughing, and expectorating that accompanied its use. The medicinal use of tobacco caught on rapidly, but soon gave way to recreational use. Its cultivation soon became more widespread. By the early 1600s there were more than 2000 tobacco plantations in south of England alone.

It was only the weakest and most palatable strains of Amerindian tobacco that were adopted by European users. Yet even these were extremely potent by today's standards: there are many accounts of deaths from excessive smoking resulting from acute nicotine poisoning. Use of tobacco at this time contrasted starkly to present-day practices. Early smokers were referred to as tobacco "drinkers" or "dry drunks," not simply because no other model than alcohol existed with which to make sense of the practice, but because the forms of tobacco in use were far more capable of inducing intoxication. In his famous *Counterblaste to Tobacco* (1604), King James I remarked that both alcohol and tobacco "stab and wound the brain with drunkenness." Some commentators at the time were concerned that smoking, like alcohol consumption, would make "men unfit for labour."

As recreational use expanded, smoking rapidly became widespread; even a mark of sociability (many tobacconists shops had the motto "Let brotherly love continue"). Smokers would meet in alehouses and coffee shops, sharing pipes and discussing the affairs of the day. The practice was typically messy: not just from filling and emptying pipes, but also in a physical sense—smoking would regularly provoke coughing, spitting, expectorating, and sometimes vomiting. With its recreationalisation, the practice also filtered down the social hierarchy; so much so that by the mid-to-late seventieth century, smoking had become "common"—it was increasingly seen as plebeian. Accordingly, from being a once fashionable practice of the higher echelons of European society, it soon came to be regarded as the mark of a dissolute lifestyle, and came to be increasingly associated with vice. There is some anecdotal evidence that by the late seventeenth century, prostitutes used the pipe as a symbol to advertise their services.

In tandem with such developments, there emerged an increasing social pressure on elite smokers to distance and distinguish their smoking practices from those of their perceived social inferiors: *a quest for distinction*, to use Elias's terminology. In relation to this development, the period witnessed the emergence of increasingly complex rituals surrounding filling pipes, lighting them, exhaling smoke, etc. Elite smoking could be distinguished from common smoking through the customs and practices that surrounded exhaling smoke, plus a kind of connoisseurship surrounding species and varies of tobacco. There also emerged a proliferation of highly prized smoking paraphernalia such as expensive pipes and jewel encrusted tobacco boxes. Historians of the period refer to "smoking dandies": highly self-conscious smokers who were subsequently somewhat ridiculed on account of their effeminate dress and slavish devotion to the latest fashions. If some accounts are to be believed, it was possible, at a price, to attend a "smoking school" where a professor in the "art" of smoking could teach you the most refined and elaborate way to consume tobacco! Gradually, however, among elite groups came to copy the French Court and adopted the practice of snuffing.

Snuffing involved the consumption of many concoctions, but generally referred to the process of snorting through the nose a quantity of powdered tobacco. Snuffing became increasingly popular in Europe of the eighteenth century. Particularly in French Aristocratic Circles, but also in Germany and England, and later in Japan and China. Snuffing is interesting because it constitutes an early example of smokeless tobacco.

There are lots of historical accounts of the nuanced and ostentatious ways of "taking the pinch": how one should show the wrist, how to offer the box of snuff to others first, and other highly complex and sophisticated codes of etiquette surrounding the practice, which would be emulated by members of the "aspiring classes". Even snuff boxes were often elaborate and ornate, made of precious metals and stones. Marie Antoinette famously would proffer snuff boxes as expensive gifts. And yet, paradoxically, while snuffing was seen to be the height of refinement, it was still incredibly messy and unsanitary by our modern standards. A good pinch of snuff would produce instant, almost violent sneezing, showering one's clothes with snot. In the case of heavy snuffers, a patina of mucous would build up over time. Again, this was still considered to be healthy. It was a way of clearing out evil humours from the head.

Snuffing was thus dangerous, not so much in the sense that we might typically understand the "dangers" of tobacco use today: it was socially dangerous. It required a skilled controlled de-controlling of the self: a rapid "escape" from and "return" to normality.

The dangers are aptly illustrated in this quote, which refers to "snuff pellets":

Snuff pellets left inside the nostrils would "draw out moisture from the nasal cavities." However, "... one only recommends it to those who, in using it, can avoid the indecency that appears when the pellets, being discharged from the nostrils and the drop of snot that is always suspended, soils the chin and nauseates the person with whom one is speaking" (Antonil 1965 [1711]: 321).

Ultimately, perhaps precisely because of these social dangers, snuff pellets did not become widely used. But they serve to illustrate the more general change of direction that is exemplified by snuff: 1) a shift towards forms of tobacco that produce short-lived, transient effects; and 2) the growing significance of fashion and changing behavioural standards—changing "sensitivities" in shaping the practices surrounding how tobacco was used.

Modern Smoking

The shift towards snuffing then, I have suggested, related to a fundamental tension: *between what tobacco does to and for us and what it does to and for others.* Perhaps the most notable thing about cigarettes—which became increasingly popular throughout the nineteenth century—was that compared to earlier modes of smoking, particularly pipe smoking, they were extremely "safe."

They were "safe" in the sense that, after a relatively short period of habituation, they generally didn't produce intoxication. Different curing processes, plus the increasing use of tobacco strains with lower yields of nicotine made cigarettes much "milder" than antecedent forms of tobacco. But that term "mildness" must be surrounded with "scare quotes." Mildness became a watchword which advertising campaigns could load with all kinds of claims: that certain cigarettes were less "irritating"; that they were milder tasting; that they were cleaner and more gentle; and also, in some cases, more genteel. Associations were drawn with "mild manners." Such associations were also highly gendered: the notion of mildness was frequently mobilised to invoke the fairer sex—associations with delicacy, lightness.

Cigarettes themselves gradually changed, continuing in the direction of the longer-term trajectory. For example, filter tips became almost ubiquitous. But these were developed not to screen out harmful chemicals, but originally to prevent the unsightly habit of spitting out loose tobacco, and to meet demands for a "less irritating" smoke. Cigarette holders too, put more distance between tobacco and the user. Again, we can see the significance of changing behavioural standards in driving changes in the form tobacco consumption takes.

Indeed, to a degree, with cigarettes the "form" of tobacco had caught up with the demands for social refinement. Cigarettes provided a much safer balance between what tobacco does to and for the user, and what it does to and for others. Compared to what came before it, the cigarette was indeed much "milder" in the sense of involving less immediately observable physical effects. While snuff was considered refined, it typically involved the expulsion of mucous, the placing of fingers into orifices, and a repeated transient loss of control through sneezing. The cigarette, by contrast, had little effect. It could even be smoked whilst working. It is paradoxical in this respect that cigarettes were in part successful precisely because their effects were much less pronounced than earlier forms of tobacco: to put it provocatively, they became successful because they "didn't do as much" to the user in an immediate and visible sense. The paradox is all the more significant with the benefit of present-day knowledge about the long-term invisible effects of tobacco consumption.

The key differences extended also to how tobacco was being used and understood by smokers. From at one stage being understood as medical agent on "the body," tobacco increasingly came to be seen as a "medicine of the mind"—a cure for the "ills" of civilisation. With the cigarette in particular, we came to understand tobacco as a psychological tool, one with "biphasic" effects: it is both a stimulant that can "pick one up," and also a sedative that can "calm one down." Tobacco, in this way, came to be understood as a substance that could be used as an *instrument of self control*: returning one to normal from different dysphoric states.

That theme of control was also increasingly extended to weight control. Slogans such as "reach for a lucky instead of a sweet" (Lucky Strike) helped reinforce the sense that smoking could make you thinner—a message that was typically aimed at female smokers. The promotion of "lighter" cigarettes at once made great play of associations with "mildness" and bodily "lightness" (weight loss). Particularly after the 1960s, lightness came to signal *lower tar* cigarettes. That trend continued with the advent of super low tar, ultra low tar, and brand variants which seemingly reduced to fractional milligrams the amount of tar and nicotine the cigarettes yielded (albeit that, as subsequent research has shown, claims that these new cigarettes were safer were spurious at best).

For present purposes, it is important to note an important shift: terms such as "mildness" and "lightness" start out at first as markers of *social* safety. They signal that a particular form of tobacco is less likely to cause embarrassment, and is more in tune with social mores. But later these terms come to be understood to be indicative of *physical* safety: of healthier, less dangerous ways to consume tobacco. This shift—from social to physical safety—is crucial for understanding subsequent developments, including the ascendancy of the electronic cigarette and its link to broader processes of civilisation.

Early-Modern to Modern Use: The Key Transitions

It is once again important to note that there are huge variations in the processes documented thus far. For example, Sweden has a long history of snuff use. Similarly, Post-Columbian North America has long association with chewing tobacco. Other forms of smokeless tobacco have at certain times and in certain places been highly significant and more than "blips" in the more general trend of smoking. That said, it is possible to discern an overall direction of change, at least at a high level of generality, which involves a series of elements.

Firstly, an overall move towards progressively less potent forms of tobacco: towards modes of consumption and species and varieties that are less likely to produce intoxication. Secondly, in tandem with this first development, we can observe a process of "diminishing degrees of pharmacological involvement." By this I refer to a kind of continuum of drugs with heavy opiates such as diacetylmorphine (heroin) on one end, and tea and coffee on the other. Tobacco, to put it crudely, has moved increasingly towards the "tea and coffee" end of this continuum in terms of its "potency," for want of a better word, for I'm referring not simply to plant yields, but also to practices surrounding use and changes in the method of its consumption. Particularly when one contrasts modern use with that of Amerindian shamans, it is possible to see how tobacco has been effectively "tamed." By this I mean that there has been a longer-term shift towards kinds of tobacco and modes of its consumption that generate less pronounced effects. Interestingly, as the "pharmacological impact" diminishes, so, increasingly have the effects of tobacco become increasingly ambiguous and open to interpretation. So in tandem with these processes we might witness a concomitant increase in "degrees of social and psychological involvement": what a tobacco user "makes" of their experience of the drug becomes progressively more significant.

The key point for present purposes is that changes in tobacco—the plant, the mode of its consumption, the practices surrounding its use, and so forth—follow changes in the social uses in tobacco. Central to these changes is the motif of *control*. To summarise it more pithily, we can over the longer term witness *a shift from the use of tobacco to lose control and escape normality and towards the use of tobacco to maintain control and return to normality.*

It is changes in the social uses of tobacco, and in relation to this, changing social and behavioural standards that have been the principal driving force for changes in tobacco use. A key factor here then is not so much growing health concerns, but growing social pressures. That is to say, concerns for *social* safety, the avoidance of social stigma, have primacy in driving developments in tobacco use. These concerns subsequently become replaced by, and conflated with concerns for *physical* safety. It is these changes that have had a major role in the shift towards cleaner, more sanitised, more "civilised" forms of tobacco.

Of course, the problem with the cigarette—*the* defining problem—was and still is that, however "refined" compared to that which came before it, it nonetheless involved smoke. That is to say, it still involved pungent fumes that invaded the air of others. Not only that, particularly over the last three decades, it has become increasingly widely accepted that this smoke is harmful not just to the person who consumes it intentionally. With this, the politics of smoking have changed dramatically. Previously, opposition to smoking had always foundered on a ethic of personal freedom: "it's my body and I can do what I want with it." But with the advent of research on the effects of second hand smoke or passive smoking, this changed: smoking became viewed as an agent of communicable disease.

Smokeless Smoking

It is against this backdrop—the shifting politics of smoking, and a sea change in public opinions towards secondary smoke—that we can understand the rise of the smokeless cigarette, a forerunner of the electronic cigarette.

One of the first was introduced was RJ Reynolds Premier, 1987. RJR, now Reynolds American, produces brands such as Camel and Winston. The Premier was lit like a normal cigarette, but it produced almost no smoke. It comprised a cylinder of tobacco wrapped around a carbon rod that was ignited and burned down. At the filter end of the cigarette were beads of tobacco extract, nicotine, and flavourings. The hot air was then drawn over these beads via inhalation. The marketing tagline for the new product was "Premier—the cleaner smoke".

Smokers hated it! They said it tasted of carbon. Despite marketing attempts to obfuscate the issue, it was not in any clear way less harmful, that is to say, physically safer, than normal smoking. It was slated at the time by tobacco control authorities for being just a piece of trickery: simply pretending to be safe. Nonetheless, my argument is that this was more than just trickery. It did indeed start to address social demands for a cigarette that was less invasive to others, which, again, must be understood against the backdrop of growing awareness of the dangers of passive smoking. It is highly significant that the marketing campaign for Premier centered on the notion that it was *cleaner*: it didn't sully the smoker—it produced less physical, moral, and aesthetic "taint."

RJR later released a similar device called Eclipse. Here the claims were that it was 90% safer than a normal cigarette. But it still contained numerous carcinogens, notably tobacco-specific nitrosamines, and other compounds such carbon monoxide. The American Cancer Society soon moved to have it outlawed, saying it created a false sense of security among smokers. This move should be understood as an extension of a more general argument developing at that time that "lighter," "low tar" variants of leading brand cigarettes had the same effect as their full tar counterparts. Rather than leading to a reduction in their consumption of harmful carcinogens by their uses, smokers would find ways to self-titrate—for example, through blocking the holes of a "Silk Cut" cigarette filter and/or taking harder "drags" from their "lites"—to obtain a higher nicotine (and with it tar) yield.

Just to be clear: this is not to dispute that the tobacco industry were often devious in the marketing of these ostensibly safer tobacco products. But rather, it is to highlight that they were also extremely adept at tapping into the longer-term set of demands for social safety and then confounding these with demands for physical safety, albeit without a scientific basis for doing so. Ultimately, neither of these devices—the Premier or the Eclipse—were successful, but they were nonetheless important antecedents of a new product that has emerged less than a decade ago: the electronic cigarette.

[...]

5

Better Definitions of Electronic Cigarettes

Public Health and Tobacco Policy Center

Public Health and Tobacco Policy Center is a New York State-funded organization that dedicates itself to improving public health through implementing evidence-based policies.

Among the many organizations established in the wake of the Master Settlement Agreement, New York's Public Health and Tobacco Policy Center provides a resource to help define exactly what an electronic cigarette is, a vital resource needed before it is possible to meaningfully regulating it. The Center notes that recent models of e-cigarettes have been designed to more closely simulate the nicotine delivery found in cigarette smoking, suggesting an approach closer to regulating cigarettes may apply.

Sustained nicotine use and addiction poses serious public health concerns. Nicotine is most commonly delivered through smoking tobacco cigarettes, which are the leading cause of preventable death in the United States. After decades of hard-earned declines in US tobacco use, a new generation is being lured to nicotine use through devices which aerosolize a solution containing the drug. These devices come in many names and forms, are hereinafter referred to as "e-cigarettes," and warrant comprehensive regulation alongside other tobacco products.

[...]

"Local Regulation of E-cigarettes," Public Health and Tobacco Policy Center, January 23, 2015. Reprinted by permission.

E-Cigarettes: The Fundamentals

What Is an E-Cigarette?

Electronic cigarettes (or "e-cigarettes") are products designed to deliver nicotine to users through inhalation without combustion (burning). While there are many names and styles for products within this category, their common feature is the ability to aerosolize liquid nicotine other substances, thus distinguishing them from products delivering nicotine through the burning of cut tobacco (e.g., cigarettes, cigars). This distinction is critical since combusted tobacco use is the overwhelming cause of tobacco-related disease and death in the United States.

For regulatory purposes, e-cigarettes have been classified as tobacco products. They entered the US market around 2007 and have quickly become popular among youth, surpassing youth cigarette use in 2014. E-cigarette manufacturers voraciously market their products, including through media and methods known to appeal to youth and kids—methods which successfully attracted youth to smoking and which the tobacco industry is now barred from employing in marketing their traditional tobacco products.

Regulating e-cigarettes is challenging: e-cigarettes are designed and sold under a number of different descriptors, such as e-hookahs, e-cigars, vape pens, personal vaporizers, electronic pipes, mods, and beyond. They are currently available in many forms and continue to evolve, sometimes eluding the definitions in policies and other controls aimed at the product category. While some states and local governments have begun to regulate e-cigarette sales and use, a standard definition for these devices remains elusive. It is therefore important to have a sense of how e-cigarettes work and some of their design variables.

At the most basic level, e-cigarettes and similar devices consist of a power source (such as a disposable or rechargeable battery, with or without variable voltage), a heating element (such as resistance wire, sometimes around wicking material or poly-fil, and housed in an "atomizer"), and reservoir (such as a disposable cartridge or refillable tank) for containing a liquid, wax, pod or gel, ("e-liquid").

E-liquid consists of, at a minimum, propylene glycol and/or glycerol and, typically, nicotine and flavorings. E-liquid can theoretically be flavor-free and/or nicotine-free; laboratory testing is typically required to determine the presence of nicotine. When the user inhales (or otherwise activates the device's heating element), the e-liquid is heated, aerosolized, and delivered to that user.

Neither the quality nor the content of e-cigarette ingredients is currently regulated, resulting in a market of wide product variation and inconsistent user experience. Moreover, the inconsistent and variable constituents include an array of carcinogens and toxicants across and within e-liquid brands and expelled aerosol.

Did You Know?

E-cigarette manufacturers are rapidly changing the design of their products in an effort to better simulate the efficient nicotine delivery of smoking.

The original, single piece disposable (closed) systems store e-liquid in a sealed reservoir (cartridge or tank) not intended to be modified or opened by the user. The sealed reservoir is designed to be discarded after it is emptied.

A rechargeable e-cigarette with a single use (disposable) cartridge is the next product, both evolutionarily and pricewise. These systems integrate the heating mechanism (housed in the "atomizer") and cartridge, or "cartomizer" in the parlance of e-cigarette consumers. Manufacturers have modified cartomizer mechanisms, improving the nicotine delivery of this closed system product category.

Closed systems sell for a relatively low price, but appear to be less a satisfactory product, and are less likely to be used by more established e-cigarette users.

Consumers are increasingly turning to rechargeable open systems with larger tank reservoirs, often refilling these tanks with e-substances customized to their preferred flavor and nicotine level. Cartomizers are now also available in refillable models, yet these devices are more commonly three-piece systems with detachable batteries, atomizers, and tanks.

"Rebuildable" models of open systems are a later development and allow further customization through the size and design of its tank, heating coils and wick, all of which influence e-liquid flow, temperature, and ultimately, the taste and volume of the aerosolized nicotine "hits" delivered by the e-cigarette.

Further, rebuildable open systems may be adapted for "dripping," whereby the user bypasses use of a reservoir and wicking materials and manually leaks e-liquid directly onto the heating coils. This process is facilitated by a drip tip—a mouthpiece that fits over the atomizer (housing the heating source)—that creates a channel through which the e-liquid flows from a manual dropper (think of eye drops) to the heat source.

Open systems are increasingly popular and quickly changing as manufacturers explore new features, especially surrounding power—which, again, influences the taste and volume of the "hit." Newer devices offer variable voltage (either automatically or manually adjustable, according to user preference) as well as LCD displays and USB ports for updating a device's internal software.

Most recently, e-cigarettes that utilize nicotine salts have overtaken the market. Nicotine salts are crystallized nicotine blended with other substances such as propylene glycol and flavorants, and they achieve a similar rate of absorption in the bloodstream as nicotine from combusted cigarettes. Popularized by the manufacturer JUUL, which features a sleek design including a removable cartridge (JUUL pod), these e-cigarettes are able to produce a larger and quicker "hit" than e-cigarettes of the past.

Where Are E-Cigarettes Sold?

E-cigarettes and similar devices are sold by traditional tobacco retailers, such as tobacconists, gas stations, bodegas, pharmacies, convenience stores, and supermarkets. They are also sold in outlets where the sale of traditional tobacco products is prohibited or not tolerated, such as the internet, shopping mall kiosks, and other mobile retailers. Further, until August 8, 2016, e-cigarette retailers have allowed free product sampling, including in indoor venues such as shopping malls. In fact, e-cigarettes have triggered a new type of business specializing in developing, selling, experimenting with, and socializing over custom e-liquid formulations, used in "open" or refillable systems. These "vape shops" are proliferating throughout the country, especially in college communities. The manner in which e-cigarettes are sold and marketed creates the impression that these products are benign and trendy. Including e-cigarettes in comprehensive tobacco control regulations is a step in correcting that impression.

Gradually, age restrictions have been placed on e-cigarette sales. As of August 8, 2016, federal law prohibits the sale of e-cigarettes to youth under age 18 and, accordingly, non-age verified sales such as those through vending machines. New York State has prohibited e-cigarette sales to youth under age 18 since 2013. New York State does not currently regulate who may sell e-cigarettes, nor does it restrict where the devices may be used. Within New York, the City of Newburgh, and Dutchess, Ulster and Cayuga counties require all tobacco retailers, including those selling e-cigarettes, to obtain a local tobacco retailer license or permit. New York City requires e-cigarette retailers to register with the city. New York City, and Suffolk, Chautauqua and Albany Counties prohibit sales of e-cigarettes (and other tobacco products) to persons under the age of 21. Additionally, New York City and many New York counties prohibit the use of e-cigarettes and similar aerosol devices everywhere smoking is prohibited.

Who Uses E-Cigarettes?

Adults and youth use e-cigarettes and use is on the rise within both populations. However, experimentation (or "ever use") is far higher among youth and young adults both nationwide and in New York. How each population uses these products, including the significant growth of youth use, may have different implications for tobacco control.

Studies of youth e-cigarette use are not easy to compare and often yield inconsistent findings on specific use patterns. Importantly and notably, research does consistently show that youth experimentation with these devices is dramatically rising. A record three million US middle and high school students reported using e-cigarettes in 2015, following a three-fold increase between 2013 and 2014 among both middle and high schoolers. In the five years e-cigarette use has been nationally measured (2011-2015), use by middle schoolers has increased nearly nine times over, and use by high schoolers has increased an astonishing ten times over. E-cigarettes are the most commonly used tobacco product among youth both nationally and in New York. The only subgroup that uses another product (cigars) at a higher rate than e-cigarettes is non-Hispanic black high school students. Low socioeconomic status is also a risk factor for adolescent e-cigarette use.

Dual electronic cigarette/traditional cigarette use is common among adolescents who currently use cigarettes and those who were not cigarette smokers previously. In New York, more than half of high school students and young adults who smoke cigarettes also use e-cigarettes or similar devices. The rate is higher nationwide, with three-quarters of current e-cigarette-using youth also identifying as cigarette smokers.

Perhaps most problematic is the rate of adolescent e-cigarette use by those who have never smoked a regular cigarette, suggesting that e-cigarettes are an initiating nicotine product. Between 2011 and 2013, the number of US students who had used e-cigarettes but never smoked tripled to a quarter million, and at least one study found that among adolescent e-cigarette experimenters, most report having never been an established smoker. Nicotine initiation through aerosol devices greatly concerns public health advocates, as youth e-cigarette use is associated with increased intention to smoke and increased cigarette smoking, including among those students who previously were nonsmokers.

Among adults, electronic cigarettes are used by current tobacco users, former tobacco users, those who have never use[d] tobacco, and those trying to quit smoking. They are also used by smokers where smoking is prohibited. Although desire to quit smoking seems to drive e-cigarette use among adults (over age 24), cessation success is unclear, and adult users (like youth users) are commonly poly or dual tobacco users, with e-cigarette/traditional cigarettes the most frequent product combination. Disturbingly, adult "never smokers" are increasingly trying and using the devices.

Smoking status, gender and age are all factors contributing to likelihood of e-cigarette use. More men than women currently use e-cigarettes (4.0 percent compared to 2.8 percent), and adult men experiment with these products at higher rates than adult women. Experimentation is highest among males, young adults (ages 18–24) and those with a history of smoking. Daily use is most typical of recent quitters and older adults, while youth daily e-cigarette use remains low.

Nationally, electronic cigarette use differs by race, national origin, and geographic region. Adult experimentation and current use is higher among American Indians or Alaska Natives and whites, than among Hispanics, non-Hispanic blacks, and non-Hispanic Asians. Adults in the Northeastern United States are significantly less likely to report current use than those in other regions. Adults with a GED are about twice as likely to report current use compared to adults with a high school diploma or higher degree.

In sum, adults and youth appear to use aerosol nicotine devices differently. Among primary e-cigarette users: 1) White youth and young adults tend to be experimental and intermittent users; and 2) Adult smokers who have recently quit tend to be daily users of e-cigarettes. Less is known about the devices' impact on longer-term cigarette and other tobacco product use within these populations.

[...]

Marketing: E-Cigarette Manufacturers Aggressively Market Their Products to Youth

Given the negative health consequences of adolescent nicotine use, the marketing practices of e-cigarette companies are especially problematic. E-cigarettes and similar devices are aggressively and—as evidenced by rising use rates among young people—successfully marketed to youth. Products that appeal to youth are available in palatable flavors and designed, packaged, priced, displayed, advertised, and otherwise marketed in a manner attractive to youth consumers.

E-cigarettes are available in a host of sweet, youth-enticing flavors, even flavors of candy and sugared breakfast cereals marketed to and popular with children. Reminiscent of youth-focused cigarette advertising shown to have caused youth cigarette initiation, e-cigarettes are widely marketed, including through all available media outlets, a heavy retail presence, celebrity endorsements, and an array of sponsorships, price promotions, and name brand merchandise. A 2015 study found that 82 percent of youth and 88 percent of young adults reported seeing e-cigarette advertising in the past year, resulting in high awareness of product marketing, particularly in the retail environment. This high advertising awareness is concurrent with rapidly rising youth e-cigarette use. A separate 2015 study found that teens who saw e-cigarette ads on TV were 43 percent more likely to say they would try the devices than those who did not see the ads.

Similar marketing tactics have been successfully used by the tobacco industry for decades to recruit youth to use combustible and smokeless tobacco products. In fact, tobacco companies marketing activities were found to have been a key factor in leading young people to take up tobacco, keep some users from quitting and increasing consumption among users. These findings paved the way for policy interventions to reduce the influence of marketing on tobacco initiation and consumption, including a legal settlement restricting tobacco advertising and promotion especially appealing to youth. The settlement restricted the very marketing activity in which e-cigarette companies currently engage, namely use of cartoons, sponsorships, outdoor and transit advertising, advertising in media and venues with high youth audience, paid product placement, name brand or logoed merchandise, and free sampling. Unsurprisingly, the three e-cigarette brands owned and marketed by major tobacco companies account for the highest advertising expenditures in 2014 (a total of $102.6 million).

6

The Future of E-Cigarette Regulation

Matt Novak

Matt Novak is the editor of Gizmodo Media's Paleofuture *blog.*

Treating electronic cigarettes just like cigarettes can be counterintuitive since the real thing is still found on shelves across the country, argues Gizmodo Media's Matt Novak. Novak also looks through the history of cigarette regulation for some indication of how e-cigarettes might be regulated, but what he finds is not good news for enthusiasts: while e-cigarettes are unlikely to go away anytime soon, they will likely become more expensive with increased regulation.

The Food and Drug Administration announced today that it wants to regulate electronic cigarettes. This isn't surprising. But there's considerable debate about what those regulations should look like. If history is any guide, the life of your average vaper (vapist? vapethusiast?) is about to get a whole lot harder.

Judging by the proposals submitted for public comment, the FDA wants to treat electronic cigarettes exactly like those olde timey cigarettes our grandparents used to smoke. But the question is, should they?

"What Tobacco's Past Means for Vaping's Future," by Matt Novak, Gizmodo Media Group, April 24, 2014. Reprinted by permission.

FDA Regulation of Tobacco Is Surprisingly New

The FDA didn't regulate tobacco until 2009. That's not a typo. The FDA had no regulatory authority over tobacco until Congress passed the Family Smoking Prevention and Tobacco Control Act in 2009.

Of course, the FDA tried to regulate tobacco before that. But after attempting to exert those powers in 1996, Brown & Williamson (then the makers of Lucky Strikes and Kools) filed suit. They made it all the way to the Supreme Court in 2000, where the court found that Congress had never intended for the FDA to regulate tobacco. A bizarre ruling indeed, but it was the law of the land for almost another decade.

Today, the FDA clearly has the authority to regulate the manufacture and sale of drugs in this country. And on their face, many of the proposals for regulating e-cigarettes—which contain nicotine, but emit vapor rather than smoke—make a lot of sense. But there are some important differences between the products that makes it foolish to treat e-cigs exactly like traditional cigarettes.

Smoke Gets in Your Eyes

As early as 1963, a patent was granted for a new kind of smokeless nicotine product. The device never made it to market, but the timing for this kind of thinking couldn't have been better. The US Surgeon General would release the first definitive government report outlining the dangers of smoking the following year.

The 1990s saw the tobacco companies experimenting with new electronic versions of their products, though they rarely got past the prototype stage. But by the beginning of the 2010s, early adopters were flocking to e-cigs due to the appeal of a nicotine delivery device, without all that nasty cancer stuff. In just a few short years, e-cigs have become a huge industry and the major tobacco companies have been buying up companies. For instance, Lorillard now owns Blu, and *Bloomberg Businessweek* projects that e-cigarettes could become a $1.5 billion industry this year.

Secondhand Vape?

The vaping backlash began long before the FDA's proposals were made public. New York City recently banned vaping in public, even in outdoor parks. Just last week, Los Angeles implemented a vaping ban in restaurants. And private businesses are largely not too keen on letting people vape, even if it's outdoors.

I recently saw a guy vaping at the San Diego Zoo, only to have a security guard approach him and say that there was no smoking allowed in the park. The poor vaper futilely tried to explain that it wasn't a real cigarette, just an e-cig. But the security guard told him it didn't matter—it still wasn't allowed.

The mere perception that someone is smoking, even if their "secondhand vapor" isn't harming anyone else, is grounds for a ban in our post-smoke acceptance world.

Rise of the Modern No-Smoking Movement

The modern mainstream anti-smoking movement has its roots in the early 1990s. By this time, the science on the health dangers of smoking was incredibly solid and grassroots anti-smoking efforts were getting much better organized. Tobacco companies were still insisting that their products were harmless, and tobacco executives even testified in front of high-profile congressional committees in 1994 claiming that they didn't believe smoking was addictive. But anti-smoking efforts were making a lot of headway. In 1995, California became the first state to ban smoking in all indoor workplaces and restaurants. By 1998, they had banned smoking in bars as well.

Public health advocates saw an opportunity in the 1990s to define indoor smoking as a workplace rights issue. Why should people working in restaurants have to be exposed to noxious poisons in the air? If that same smoke with the exact same carcinogens was coming from some machine in the corner of the bar, rather than from patrons' cigarettes, would the government allow it?

In 1994, the tobacco control community saw OSHA as their best shot at banning tobacco indoors across the country. If the FDA didn't have the authority to regulate tobacco use on the federal level, then maybe OSHA could as a workplace safety issue. But labor unions were quick to scuttle that idea. The old guard of chain-smoking union guys weren't about to be told that they had to put their cigarettes out. And the tobacco control community eventually realized that they had a better chance at fighting cigarettes on the local level.

Perhaps the most overlooked aspect of the rise of anti-smoking laws has a lot to do with California being the first to ban it. Countless people moved away from the populous state after 1995 only to be shocked that smoking was allowed in the bars and restaurants of their new home states. The societal norms were shifting, in no small part because mobile Californians had simply gotten used to not going home smelling like smoke after having a dinner out.

Flavors, Flavors, Everywhere

The FDA seems concerned that e-cigs will be (or are currently being) marketed to minors. This is a valid concern, if you look back at the history of tobacco marketing.

In the 1970s, the major tobacco companies and their advertising agencies explored all kinds of different ideas to attract youths to smoking. Like in the memo above, where Brown & Williamson's marketing firm wondered if honey cigarettes would be a good idea since, "It's a well known fact that teenagers like sweet products."

Today, e-cigs come in a variety of flavors, which adults certainly consume. But there's a reasonable case to be made that flavored vaping could contribute to the rise of use by children. This is one area where the FDA should certainly do more research.

A Double-Edged Sword for Tobacco Companies

Most tobacco companies resisted regulation by the FDA until the 2000s, largely because they were afraid that smoking would be outlawed. And this was a reasonable concern. How could a product that kills hundreds of thousands of people each year be left on the market? If one in three people who used a mop eventually died from mop-related illnesses, you could make a pretty compelling case to ban mops.

Interestingly, the largest tobacco company was just fine with regulation. By the late 1990s, Philip Morris was A-OK with the FDA regulating tobacco because it established some forms of legal protection for the product. Not coincidentally, the tobacco industry was in the middle of getting hammered by lawsuits from states who were upset that they were footing the bill for smoking related illnesses.

Not surprisingly, Lorillard (the owner of Blu e-cigs) released a statement today saying that they support the FDA's efforts to regulate the product in a reasonable manner. Lorillard seems confident that e-cigs will prove safe, and emphasize a "science-based approach" to the issue.

"It appears that the FDA is taking a science-based approach, and that the proposed rule itself defines a constructive process that recognizes that e-cigarettes are different than combustible cigarettes," the CEO of Lorillard said. "Despite what I am sure will be a robust give-and-take process over the comings months, we remain committed to our belief that electronic cigarettes represent a major opportunity to align the interests of business and public health."

Regulation means validation. And should e-cigs suddenly cause everybody to grow a second nose on their elbows or something, Lorillard welcomes the opportunity to point at government regulators having approved the product as safe for public consumption by adults.

What's the Harm in Harm Reduction?

The American public health community has always been uncomfortable with harm reduction. But harm reduction is an important consideration when you live in a dangerous world filled with all kinds of wonderfully harmful drugs. The idea is that if people are going to do damage to their bodies, why not set public health policies that allow for people to reduce the damage done?

It's the same concept that drives more progressive communities to embrace needle exchange programs or crack pipe vending machines, as they recently installed in Vancouver. Harm reduction products, like e-cigs, allow people who want to consume nicotine a more healthy alternative.

However, the FDA seems poised to revert to puritanical notions of all or nothing when it comes to nicotine use, when we read between the lines of their proposal. Everything about the proposals point toward treating them as cigarettes. Even though research already points to e-cigs being a useful alternative for smokers that could lead to fewer smoking deaths in the long term.

It's the Future, So Where's My Safer Cigarette?

Nicotine is a drug. And as such, there's nothing wrong with the government making sure that this particular drug is safe for public consumption, and short of that, ensuring that people know what they're putting in their bodies.

For years, people switched to "light" cigarettes thinking that they were safer. But they weren't. The FDA banned the use of "light" as a designation for cigarettes, and now, if you want a pack of Camel Lights, you need to get Camel Blue. This seems reasonable, if a bit confusing.

The tricky thing with e-cigs is that they've been on the market for a relatively short period of time. While there's virtually no question that vaping is safer than smoking cigarettes, there's still the "what if" crowd to contend with.

Vape 'em if you got 'em, because e-cigarettes aren't going away any time soon. But they're almost certainly about to become much more expensive, and much more difficult to find—if only because they're merely associated with smoking. Which is a shame. Because ironically, treating e-cigs like traditional smokes could wind up needlessly contributing to smoking-related deaths.

7

Electronic Cigarettes Urge Consensus

Jamie Hartmann-Boyce

Jamie Hartmann-Boyce is a senior researcher in health behaviors and managing editor of the Cochrane Tobacco Addiction Review Group.

Jamie Hartmann-Boyce and other researchers develop the argument that electronic cigarettes are a viable alternative to cigarettes, using the profound evidence of cigarettes' health risks to advocate for anything else by default. But she holds back on endorsing electronic cigarettes outside the context of replacing the larger social ill. "In general, it's not a great idea to inhale chemicals into your lungs if you can avoid it," Hartmann-Boyce writes. With the uptick in research on e-cigarettes, Hartmann-Boyce believes that a consensus will soon be reached on the effects and risks of vaping.

Earlier this year, Michael Gove claimed Britain's had enough of experts. Now I don't agree with Gove on much, but when it comes to e-cigarettes, he may have a point. We're bombarded with stories about these products, but most just add to the confusion, with perceptions of vaping risks rising year on year. Just recently the *Sun* informed us that experts are saying "e-cigs are just as bad for your heart as smoking fags," but read a couple lines down and you'll find other experts reasserting the claim that e-cigarettes are 95% safer than tobacco. So which is it? Why can't the scientists agree? And will they ever?

"Why Can't Scientists Agree on E-Cigarettes?" by Jamie Hartmann-Boyce, Guardian News and Media Limited, September 14, 2016. Reprinted by permission.

Cochrane is a global non-profit group that reviews all the evidence on healthcare interventions and summarises the findings so people making important decisions—you, your doctor, the people who write medical guidelines—can use unbiased information to make difficult choices without having to first read every study out there. This week, the latest Cochrane review of e-cigarettes was published. I'm its lead author. While our conclusions are limited because there aren't many high quality studies available yet, overall the evidence suggests that (1) e-cigarettes with nicotine can help people quit smoking, (2) they don't seem to have any serious side effects in the short- to mid-term (up to 2 years), and (3) in some cases, switching to them leads to changes in your blood and breath that are consistent with the changes you'd see in people who give up smoking altogether.

This is good news. But other systematic reviews and studies have drawn very different conclusions, and I'm going to try to shed some light why that is.

Can E-Cigarettes Help People Quit?

Our Cochrane review suggests they can. But a review published in the *Lancet Respiratory Medicine* earlier this year, which received a lot of attention, suggests they actually make it harder. The reason for this difference is the types of studies the authors include.

Randomized controlled trials are the best way to see if a treatment works. As Ben Goldacre, author of *Bad Science*, explains, by randomly assigning people to one intervention or another and measuring the outcome in the same way across both groups, you can rule out alternative explanations for differences between groups. The reviews that find e-cigarettes help people quit smoking only include randomized controlled trials. The studies (like this one and this one) that find that e-cigarettes *stop* people from quitting aren't randomized controlled trials—instead they survey smokers and ask if they are using e-cigarettes. Then, some months later, they ask the same people if they are still smoking. We don't know if the results from these studies reflect the effect of vaping, or if something else about the vapers makes it harder for them to quit. For example, it might be reasonable to imagine they are more dependent smokers, which is why they vape as well as using regular cigarettes. This would make quitting harder.

Are They Safe?

The issue here isn't so much the study type, but the way you ask the question. By "safe," do you mean completely without risk? No, they're not—not much is. We've seen stories about people catching fire and puppies with nicotine poisoning. Plus, in general, it's not a great idea to inhale chemicals into your lungs if you can avoid it. Experts basically agree on that—I've yet to come across a tobacco researcher or policy maker who would recommend you start using e-cigarettes if you aren't already a smoker.

The crucial question here is—safe compared to what? Cigarettes are uniquely deadly. They kill one in two people who use them regularly. So, if you're asking whether e-cigarettes are safer than regular cigarettes, most experts would, after briefly hesitating, lean on the side of yes. The hesitation is there because e-cigarettes are new to the scene. We don't know their long-term safety profile, so we have to look for clues elsewhere—for example, studies that measure side effects of short-term use (results from these are promising) and studies about how e-cigarettes affect your blood, lungs and heart. Interpreting these measures is complicated. For example, a recent study found that vaping affects the same blood vessel in your heart as smoking regular cigarettes. This isn't necessarily surprising—we know nicotine, the active agent in both, affects this vessel. We also know that nicotine isn't responsible for the harms associated with smoking. So how to interpret these results? The gamut of expert reactions ran from "[e-cigarettes are] far more dangerous than people realise" to "vaping carries a fraction of the risk of smoking." When it comes to long-term safety, experts are making their best guesses in the absence of solid data, and that's where room for disagreement creeps in.

So What's Next?

The good news is there's lots of research going on—finally. The most recent update of the Cochrane review found 26 studies in the pipeline that will help answer questions about the safety and effect of using e-cigarettes to quit smoking. The more studies we have looking at a question, the more certain we can be about the answer. The irony is that until we have the answer, narrow interpretations of the results of individual studies risk doing further harm, undermining public confidence in science and possibly discouraging quit attempts. Fundamentally, tobacco researchers on both sides of the argument want the same thing—to reduce death and disease. We're in the same boat. If you're reading this as a member of the public, please don't be put off by the conflicting headlines—we all agree cigarettes are bad for you, most of us agree vaping is probably *much* safer than smoking regular cigarettes, and if you're a smoker we all really want our research to help you to quit. Don't let us get in the way.

8

Regulation: Possibly Bad

Jeff Stier and Henry I. Miller

Jeff Stier is a senior fellow at the Consumer Choice Center and Henry I. Miller is the Robert Wesson Fellow in Scientific Philosophy and Public Policy at Stanford University's Hoover Institution.

In a piece published by the conservative National Review, *electronic cigarette advocates found an ally in the hard choice logic of the consumer-driven health model. Jeff Stier and Henry I. Miller frame the conversation about electronic cigarettes around them as delivery agents of the opportunity to quit. In this model, the health hazard of cigarettes is a market problem and electronic cigarettes are a market solution. Because of the obvious and immediate benefits compared to cigarettes, they argue that less study and regulation is needed. The market can take it from here.*

H arm reduction—opting for a product or activity that is not harmless but is better than the existing alternative—is a common and obvious strategy that we employ almost unthinkingly. For example, many drugs used for chemotherapy to treat cancer are highly toxic and cause a variety of serious side effects, but taking them is better than leaving the cancer untreated.

Another example is the substitution of lower-risk nicotine products, such as electronic "cigarettes" that deliver nicotine in vapor form, for tobacco cigarettes. Because there is no combustion,

"Promote Health by Not Defending the E-Cigarette Ban," by Jeff Stier and Henry I. Miller, *National Review*, May 16, 2017. Reprinted by permission. © National Review, Inc. 2018.

using these devices ("vaping") is intrinsically less dangerous than cigarettes—95 percent less harmful, according to Public Health England—and they can help adults to quit smoking.

England's Royal College of Physicians urged doctors last year to "promote the use of e-cigarettes, NRT [nicotine replacement therapy] and other non-tobacco nicotine products as widely as possible as a substitute for smoking in the UK," because they provide "nicotine without the smoke." And Professor Michael Russell, whose research was the foundation for the 1988 US Surgeon General's report on nicotine addiction, said simply: "People smoke for nicotine but they die from the tar."

Yet in the United States, FDA regulations are denying smokers the opportunity to use e-cigarettes to quit. Further complicating the landscape, leading public-health groups, including the American Heart Association, the American Lung Association, and the American Cancer Society, are actively lobbying against e-cigarettes and misrepresenting the science about both the safety of e-cigarettes and how they can help cigarette smokers significantly reduce their risk. Local governments are behaving just as badly. Consider this outrageously unscientific ad campaign that the New York State Department of Health is sponsoring in *U.S. News and World Report.*

Although anti-e-cigarette activists claim that it will take decades to know whether e-cigarettes are less harmful than smoking, we already know a great deal about why cigarette smoking is so devastatingly dangerous: It is primarily due to the combustion of tobacco.

We also know a tremendous amount about e-cigarettes, the liquid that goes into them, and what comes out and is inhaled. Are we sure they are all completely "safe"? No. But there's no question that they are far less harmful than cigarettes, the most dangerous, irredeemable, widely used consumer product ever invented. And we know that many smokers are using them to quit.

Earlier this month, partisan politics in the Senate blocked an effort to rein in the FDA's retroactive de facto ban on e-cigarettes, known as the "deeming" regulation. The legislative fix, as outlined in the bipartisan Cole-Bishop rider to the budget bill, was a modest but urgent effort to fix part of the Obama administration's ban. The amendment would have restricted the FDA's new "deeming" regulations and its ill-conceived "pre-market tobacco application" process to e-cigarette products that first went on sale on or after August 8, 2016 (the date the deeming rule took effect), with those introduced before that date (which includes almost all e-cigarette products) being allowed to remain on the market under the preexisting regulations.

The Cole-Bishop amendment was approved by the House Agriculture Appropriations Committee, and was on its way to becoming law via the budget bill. But Senate Democrats threatened a government shutdown if this and a range of other legislative riders were included in the legislation.

The same day the budget was unveiled, the FDA announced an extension to deadlines related to the deeming regulations. In an e-mail to stakeholders, the agency said the extensions "will allow new leadership at the FDA and the Department of Health and Human Services additional time to more fully consider issues raised by the final rule that are now the subject of multiple lawsuits in federal court."

Newly confirmed FDA commissioner Dr. Scott Gottlieb and the Justice Department can now consider the prospects and policy implications of defending the Obama FDA's flawed regulatory process, which is facing six different lawsuits at various stages, with more in the offing.

What are the government's chances of defeating all the increasingly expensive and expansive challenges? It's certainly not even close to being a sure thing.

Consider just one example. Does Attorney General Jeff Sessions propose, in good faith, to defend the many absurdities put forth in the rule, as laid out in Obama-era court filings? For instance, the Obama administration contended that vaping devices alone, which don't even contain consumable liquid (it's sold separately) and are widely used by former smokers who vape with zero-nicotine liquid, are in fact "tobacco products" under the Tobacco Control Act. Surely AG Sessions doesn't believe this contorted approach necessary to justify the rule. He shouldn't think the courts will either.

The policy implications of "winning" in court are even more clear. There would be a retroactive and innovation-stifling regulation that would decimate an entire class of life-saving products.

Taking all this into account, the Trump administration now has a unique opportunity to make good on its promise to roll back the worst of the Obama-era regulations, by undoing one that won't only kill American jobs but will kill Americans.

How would it do so?

There's one approach to reversing the rule that would obviate the need for ponderous rulemaking or the uncertain legislative process: The Justice Department could decline to continue to defend the deeming regulation in court. If the department ceased to defend it against the many viable legal challenges, the rule would either be nullified by a court or else be scaled back by way of a broad-based consent decree. A judicially approved consent decree could leave in place certain aspects of the rule, such as the ban on sales to minors, that are not a matter of dispute.

Gottlieb might be tempted to simply refrain from enforcing the rule, but this approach would be perilous not only because of political considerations, but because it would leave the rule in place for a future administrator to enforce. The innovative and young vaping industry, already under misguided attacks, urgently needs predictability.

Rolling back the regulation through a new rule-making process would also be a major step in the right direction, but that course would entail unnecessary political risks by nakedly second-guessing a rule already in place. The administration will be on firmer political, legal, and practical footing if it exercises its discretion to evaluate the current status and merits of the legal cases it is being asked to defend. Critics will howl, but they'll be criticizing an approach that Obama deftly used as a tactic when his Justice Department decided not to defend duly passed legislation it determined not to be legally defensible (the Defense of Marriage Act). In fact, declining to defend a law that an administration considers indefensible, and that was enacted by a different branch of the government, should be held to a higher standard than an executive-branch decision not to defend a rule enacted by the executive branch, albeit in a previous administration. This is especially so when there is a legitimate question whether the rule was in fact duly enacted, as is the case here, and when many of the legal challenges center on whether the enactment of the rule complied with administrative law.

In his Senate confirmation hearing, Gottlieb alluded to this, perhaps prophetically, in response to questions about how to balance the benefit of e-cigarettes against any risk. "I think a properly constructed and overseen regulatory *process* [emphasis added] should have the capacity under the authorities Congress gave the agency to make these determinations," he said.

The Obama FDA's process was improperly constructed and lacked effective oversight. Declining to defend the process by which the rule was created would also give Congress time to rethink the underlying 2009 Tobacco Control Act, which did not even contemplate e-cigarettes, a class of disruptive-technology products that was in an early stage of development at the time.

Gottlieb also stated, "We need to make sure we're getting the most bang for our regulatory buck." Spending the Justice Department's and the FDA's already stretched resources on defending the indefensible is hardly a good investment.

Attorney General Sessions, in consultation with Commissioner Gottlieb, can act right now by announcing the administration's decision not to further defend the myriad cases. Not only would doing so remove a politically charged issue from Gottlieb's already very full plate, but it would help to restore the FDA's credibility. It would also prevent DOJ from being forced to make untenable legal arguments. Most important of all, it would save the lives of smokers who would like to quit, today and in the future.

9

Electronic Cigarettes Can Do No Wrong

Public Health England

Public Health England is a government agency that is part of the Department of Health and Social Care in the United Kingdom.

This 2015 study by Public Health England on electronic cigarette use strongly asserts that there are limited risks in using the devices. The government agency concludes that regular use among never-smokers is rare based on local study pools, and as such, the focus should be on the positive benefits to smokers rather than the risk of causing non-smokers to begin smoking. The report also takes aim at a log of the less-positive language used in the larger conversation about addiction—to nicotine or other such substances. They assert that "Gateway Theory" is often misused in conversation about electronic cigarettes. In fact, it is "rather more complicated."

In England, EC [electronic cigarettes] first appeared on the market within the last 10 years and around 5% of the population report currently using them, the vast majority of these smokers or recent ex-smokers. Whilst there is some experimentation among never smokers, regular use among never smokers is rare. Cigarette smoking among youth and adults has continued to decline and there is no current evidence

"E-Cigarettes: An Evidence Update. A Report Commissioned by Public Health England," by McNeill A, Brose LS, Calder R, Hitchman SC, Hajek P and McRobbie H, Public Health England, August 2015. https://assets.publishing.service.gov.uk/government/uploads/system/uploads/attachment_data/file/457102/Ecigarettes_an_evidence_update_A_report_commissioned_by_Public_Health_England_FINAL.pdf. Licensed Under CC by 3.0.

in England that EC are renormalising smoking or increasing smoking uptake. Instead, the evidence reviewed in this report point in the direction of an association between greater uptake of EC and reduced smoking, with emerging evidence that EC can be effective cessation and reduction aids.

Regulations have changed little in England since the previous PHE reports with EC being currently governed by general product safety regulations which do not require products to be tested before being put on the market. However, advertising of EC is now governed by a voluntary agreement and measures are being introduced to protect children from accessing EC from retailers. Manufacturers can apply for a medicinal licence through the Medicines and Healthcare products Regulatory Agency (MHRA) and from 2016, any EC not licensed by the MHRA will be governed by the revised European Union Tobacco Products Directive (TPD).

[...]

Introduction

Despite the decline in smoking prevalence observed over the last few decades, there remain over eight million smokers in England. Most of these are from manual and more disadvantaged groups in society, including those with mental health problems, on low income, the unemployed and offenders. In some such population groups, the proportion who smoke is over two or three times higher than that in the general population, a level of smoking observed in the general population over 40 years ago. For those who continue to smoke regularly, much of their lives will be of lower quality and spent in poorer health than those who don't smoke, and they will have a one in two chance of dying prematurely, by an average of 10 years, as a direct result of their smoking. Smoking is therefore the largest single contributor to health inequalities as well as remaining the largest single cause of preventable mortality and morbidity in England.

Moving forward, it is therefore important to maintain and enhance England's comprehensive tobacco control strategy in order to motivate and support all smokers in society to stop smoking as quickly as possible, and prevent the recruitment of new smokers. Harm reduction guidance, published by the National Institute for Health and Care Excellence in England in 2013, recognised that some smokers struggled to quit abruptly and that cigarettes were a lethal delivery system for nicotine; it is widely accepted that most smokers smoke for the nicotine but die from the other smoke constituents. Harm reduction has been identified as one of the more promising policy options to reduce smoking induced inequalities in health. All experts agree that a well-resourced comprehensive strategy, involving cessation, prevention and harm reduction should make the goal of a smoke-free society in England quickly achievable.

However, the advent of electronic cigarettes (EC) over recent years has caused controversy. In 1991, Professor Michael Russell, a leading English smoking cessation expert from the Institute of Psychiatry, argued that "it was not so much the efficacy of new nicotine delivery systems as temporary aids to cessation, but their potential as long-term alternatives to tobacco that makes the virtual elimination of tobacco a realistic future target," and he recommended that "tobacco should be rapidly replaced by cleaner, less harmful, sources of nicotine." Professor Russell was one of the first to recognise the critical role that nicotine played in tobacco use and he identified that whilst there were good ethical and moral reasons not to promote nicotine addiction in society, the harm caused by nicotine was orders of magnitude lower than the harms caused by cigarette smoke. Professor Russell was also a pioneer of new treatments for smoking cessation, in particular, nicotine replacement therapies (NRT). Since then, the number of NRT products has proliferated such that there are now several different delivery routes and modes and countless different dosages and flavours. However, even with a relaxation of the licensing restrictions which increased their accessibility, NRT products have never become popular as an alternative to smoking.

In 2004, the first EC was marketed in China, and EC started to appear in England in 2006/7. The subsequent three years saw a rapid rise in their use. Whilst Professor Russell died in 2009, predating the arrival of these products in England, proponents of EC similarly recognised their potential to contribute towards making a smoke-free society more rapidly achievable. Those against EC, however, believed that they were at best a distraction, at worst a means of undoing decades of progress in reducing smoking.
[…]

Use of E-Cigarettes Among Young People

In 2015, the ASH survey found that 12.7% of 11 to 18-year olds reported having tried EC; of these, 80.9% had only used one once or twice (10.2% of all respondents). Current EC use was considerably lower: 0.7% had used an EC sometimes but not more than once a month; 1.2% more than once a month but not weekly; and 0.5% weekly. The prevalence of EC use (2.4% overall) among people aged between 11 and 18 was therefore lower than among the general population. In comparison, 21% of all 11 to 18-year olds reported having tried cigarettes, of whom 54% only tried once (11.4% of all respondents). Current smoking was reported by a total of 6.7%; 2.7% smoked less than weekly and 4% at least weekly.

Experimentation increased with age: 2.9% of 11-year olds and 20.2% of 18-year olds had tried EC. In comparison, among 11-year olds, 3.9% had tried cigarettes (0.7% current smokers), whereas 40.9% of 18-year olds had tried cigarettes (14.3% current smokers).

Use of EC was very closely linked with smoking status. Among never smokers, 0.3% used EC monthly or more often, compared with 10.0% of ever smokers and 19.1% of current smokers. The majority of EC users had tried tobacco cigarettes first.
[…]

Controlling for other variables associated with EC use, parental use of EC and peer smoking remained significantly associated with having ever used an EC. Having ever used an EC was associated with weaker anti-smoking intentions. Parental EC use was not associated with weakened anti-smoking intentions whereas parental smoking was. This study, published prior to the one above, concluded that EC represented a new form of experimentation with nicotine that was more common than tobacco usage. It also commented that the findings added "some tentative support for the hypothesis that use of e-cigarettes may increase children's susceptibility to smoking." However, as this was a cross-sectional survey, causal connections cannot be inferred. It is possible that children who had used EC would have smoked cigarettes in their absence and this could explain the relationship between intentions and EC usage.

[...]

Recent Trends in Smoking Prevalence

Since EC arrived on the market in England, smoking prevalence has continued to decline among both adults and youth. Evidence to date therefore conflicts with any suggestion that EC are renormalising smoking. Whilst other factors may be contributing to the decline in smoking, it is feasible that EC may be contributing to reductions in smoking over and above any underlying decline.

Gateway

The gateway theory or hypothesis is commonly invoked in addiction discourse, broadly to suggest that the use of one drug (sometimes a legal one such as tobacco or alcohol) leads to the use of another drug (sometimes an illegal one) but its definition is contested. No clear provenance exists and its origin appears to derive from lay, academic and political models. It is apparent that discussions about the natural progression of drug use observed in longitudinal studies of young people appear to have morphed into implicit conclusions on causality without any evidential backing. Some have argued that the effect could be causal if the use of one drug, biochemically or pharmacologically, sensitises the brains of users to the rewarding effects of other drugs making the dependent use of these other drugs more likely. However, there are many plausible competing hypotheses for such a progression including i) shared networks and opportunities to purchase the drugs; and ii) individual characteristics such as genetic predispositions or shared problematic environment. Academic experts have stated that the gateway concept "has been one of the most controversial hypotheses ... in part because proponents and opponents of the hypothesis have not always been clear about what the hypothesis means and what policies it entails." Indeed, a recent analysis of gateway concluded "Although the concept of the gateway theory is often treated as a straightforward scientific theory, its emergence is rather more complicated. In effect, it is a hybrid of popular, academic and media accounts—a construct retroactively assembled rather than one initially articulated as a coherent theory."

Despite these serious and fatal flaws in the arguments, the use of the term "gateway" is commonplace both in the academic literature and the lay press, particularly in relation to EC use and whether EC are a gateway to smoking. Some have suggested that if EC use increases at the same time as smoking increases then EC are acting as a gateway to smoking. Similarly, it's been argued that if someone uses an EC first and then initiates smoking, EC are a gateway. These arguments are clearly erroneous. To give one example of the misuse of the gateway concept, a BMJ news item on the Moore et al., 2014 cross-sectional study discussed above commented that "[EC] could be a gateway into smoking."

10

The Social Factors of Vaping

Jason Hughes

Jason Hughes is head of the department of media, communication, and sociology at the University of Leicester in the United Kingdom. His recent research has focused extensively on e-cigarette usage among young people.

Once the history of electronic cigarettes is pulled out of the larger story of the tobacco culture that it fits into, Hughes details the social history of the electronic cigarette, using that logic to approach some of the larger questions hanging over the budding industry. Are they a new kind of cigarette or cigarette replacement? Therapy device or medication? He argues that the answers to these questions cannot be found in the technical aspects of the product, smoke, or vapor, but in a rigorous study of its social uses, some of which he has conducted himself.

E lectronic cigarettes are now known in policy circles as "ENDs": electronic nicotine delivery systems. For the benefit of those who have never seen or used an electronic cigarette, here's a brief description. The device contains a battery, an atomiser, a heating element and a replaceable cartridge. They contain no "tobacco" as such, just its principal derivative, nicotine, suspended in a propylene glycol liquid solution (sometimes in glycerine and water). When heated, that turns into a fine smoke-like mist or "vapour" (users

"E-Cigarettes and the 'Civilising' of Smoking," by Jason Hughes, Cambio: Rivista sulle Trasformazioni Sociali, June 2014. http://www.fupress.net/index.php/cambio/article/view/19241/17866. Licensed under CC BY 4.0.

are called "vapers" on this basis). Vaping looks like smoking, but involves not combustion, just atomization: steam, not smoke. It is currently possible to buy many different flavours of the nicotine solution—cherry, coffee, toffee, vanilla, bubble gum, even tobacco! Some have LEDs at one end, again glowing in a way that simulates smoking. So for the first time, smokers truly have a means of *"smoking without smoke."*

According to some estimates [provided by Action on Smoking and Health (ASH) in 2014], there are something like 1.3 million e-cigarette users in the UK alone. That is still a fraction of the 10 million people who smoke. But the number has grown rapidly over the last few years. (Two years ago it was only 500,000). One of the first ever e-cigarettes was developed in the US as far back as 1963, but it emerged at a time when conventional cigarette use was still on the rise. Quite some time later, the "Ruyan" was brought to market (in 2005) by a Chinese electronics start up. Ruyan received a patent in 2007. Since then, rapid changes have been underway. E-cigarettes have increasingly come to be publicly noticed and debated. Over the last year in particular, there has been an explosion of interest in the popular and scientific literature.

Key developments in the rise of e-cigarettes include a move away from the straightforward mimicking of conventional cigarettes. There are now a bewildering array of futuristic looking devices, some of which bear no resemblance to ordinary cigarettes. Many authors now draw a distinction between first generation devices, which are "cig-a-likes" (a portmanteau of cigarette lookalikes) and second generation devices, which tend to look very little like conventional cigarettes and have refillable nicotine solution reservoirs. Second generation devices generally deliver more nicotine and are more customisable by users. They mark a further stage in the much longer-term individualisation of smoking. Another significant development is the increasing involvement of large tobacco corporations. Reynolds American has recently brought to mark the Vuse. The Vuse marketing pitch includes an explanation of why it is the "World's most advanced e-cigarette": "The VaporDelivery processor working with SmartMemory monitors and adjusts the power and heat up to 2,000 times a second … ensuring consistently satisfying puffs" (vusevapor.com). Reynolds is clearly beginning to draw upon its expertise in having a long history of making cigarettes to "ensure satisfaction" for the latter day "tobacco" consumer. Similarly Altria Group (maker of Marlboro cigarettes) has introduced Mark Ten, a very modern, clean sleek looking product with space-age packaging to match. Such products are seemingly a world away from iconic adverts featuring the Marlboro Man—the rugged cowboy looking out across the vast expanse of Western wilderness.

We might then be tempted to see the rise of smokeless smoking as a very recent development, but in fact, smokeless tobacco devices have already been with us for quite some time. We tend not to think of them as such, but nicotine replacement therapies (NRTs) have been around since the 1980s. Something like 1-in-3 smokers have tried them, and many continue to use them as alternatives to cigarettes rather than as cessation devices.

Nicotine as a Therapy or a Drug?

Nicotine replacement therapies include patches, gum, sprays, lozengers, and the "inhalator"—a device that looks like a plastic cigarette, a tube through which nicotine and air can be "sucked."

It is significant that, in the mind of policy makers, for a long-time there has been widespread acceptance of the clear difference between these therapies that help us *stop* smoking, and tobacco products that help us *keep* smoking. But the rise of e-cigarettes has now blurred this distinction beyond all meaningful recognition. The distinction relates to a long-running debate in tobacco control circles: between those who favour abstention and those who favour safer sources of nicotine. In recent years, ASH, the Royal College of Physicians, and other key authorities have increasingly come to accept a harm reduction strategy, but this remains highly contentious.

So what we have witnessed, effectively, is a convergence of devices to stop smoking with new modes of consuming tobacco. To return to my opening question: how can we explain this? How did this come to be? Here we come to some key sociological theories. The most significant of which is "medicalisation."

Medicalisation

Tobacco, if anything, is an archetypical case of medicalisation. The term refers to the extension of medical jurisdiction over increasingly broader areas of people's lives. This involves a shift in how behaviours such as smoking are understood, classified, and "treated" (in both senses)—a shift from "badness" to "sickness" as sociologists [Peter] Conrad and [Joseph W.] Schneider (1980) put it. With this shift, we have seen the growing understanding of tobacco as an addictive disease in itself, and with it, a shift in the social opposition to tobacco: from being a sign of immorality or a dissolute lifestyle, towards it being understood as a public health risk.

But a simple reading of medicalisation does not fit so well with the historical evidence. The medical profession—and it is problematic to talk about the profession as though it constituted a homogeneous group—has, for the longest time, had a complex relationship with tobacco. For instance, there are many well-documented cases of individual GPs privately endorsing smoking to calm the nerves, even some time after the epidemiological studies by [Richard] Doll and [A. Bradford] Hill linking smoking to lung cancer (1950). Even a very recent study by Alison Pilnick and Tim Coleman (2010) found the profession at best circumspect in accepting the delegation of responsibility for smoking. The study examined clinical encounters between doctors and patients who seek advice on smoking cessation, and found that GPs shied away from pressure to practice preventative medicine in the form of prescribing NRTs, and from framing the problem as squarely one for medical jurisdiction. In addition, there is evidence to suggest that some pharmaceutical companies have been hesitant to become involved in NRTs because of the potential damage an association with tobacco might do their public image.

However, if we adopt a broader view of medicalisation: as, to put it simply, about the extension of medical "frames of reference," the evidence and case is rather more compelling. Particularly since Michael Russell's work in the 1970s, we have come to think of smoking as *essentially a means of nicotine self-administration*. Russell's work established the idea that smokers become addicted to nicotine, but get killed by the tar in cigarettes. To this day, this core idea underpins the search for safer sources of nicotine, and eventually, NRTs.

So my argument is that medical understandings of tobacco haven't just changed how we think about tobacco, they've helped drive a change in what "tobacco" actually is: users increasingly no longer consume tobacco, they consume instead its principal derivative "nicotine." This involves a kind of self-fulfilling prophecy: we come to think of tobacco use as simply nicotine self-administration and this, over the longer term, has helped tobacco use *become* essentially a form of nicotine self-administration. Tobacco has become pharmacologically and socially "sanitised," cleansed of its "dirty" compounds—reduced to just its principal psychoactive component nicotine, suspended in liquid. And even lay understandings of tobacco use have followed suit: smokers and vapers understand themselves as "nicotine users," and tobacco use as a practice is widely recognised as "nicotine addiction." It hardly needs to be stated that we no longer think of tobacco use as a "private habit," or a "collective ritual": we understand it in medical terms and frames of reference. Policies, practices and patterns of use follow directly from that set of understandings.

Paradoxically, both e-cigarettes and NRTs, when viewed in this fundamental way, *are exactly the same thing*s: nicotine administration systems. So the emergence and increasing dominance of medical understandings of tobacco use has left a gaping, quite beautiful, but also quite contradictory, tautology. This is nowhere better illustrated than in the case of NRTs: here we have a therapy that is based on the idea that *we can use nicotine to "treat" tobacco*. But with the rise of e-cigarettes, "tobacco" has effectively *become* just "nicotine." So, again, *what now is the difference between the devices we use to keep smoking and the devices we use to stop smoking*? There's a distinction in policy debates between "medicinal nicotine" and smokeless tobacco products: one is a "therapy," the other is a "drug." But this distinction is, in the final analysis, pure artifice. When one consults users, the distinction completely collapses.

Physical or Social Safety?

Here's an extract from a contributor's post to a UK forum for "vapers":

> *Got my E-cig, a pleasantly sophistomacated looking gadget … it gives excellent vaper … To be honest, I think the government should push em: The product is sold to you with no suggestion of it being a smoking (nicotine) cessation device. I'm enjoying switching my addiction delivery to the E-cig, and not gum or patches. And I get to blow vaper in the pub. Lovely :)—ProppyGander*

For ProppyGander this is simply another way of "smoking." She has internalised the medicalised idea that this is a "nicotine delivery system," indeed this clearly informs how she thinks about what it is that she is doing: but she was already using gum/patches in this way too. In this sense, e-cigarettes are a have your cake and eat it device from a user's perspective. Essentially, they provide both "physical" and "social" safety: th*ey won't kill me, and I can carry on smoking: I can even smoke in the pub.*

To put it provocatively, the distinction between nicotine the therapy and nicotine the drug is one that is drawn in the air, so to speak. Unlike methadone and diacetylmorphine (the therapy to treat the drug—heroin), NRTs and e-cigarettes deliver exactly the same alkaloid: the same substance. There are two key points for the purposes of this discussion. 1) Viewed in the longer-term, the rise of NRTs and e-cigarettes are actually two sides of the same coin, that is to say, two facets of the same development.

The development, over the longer-term, has been the increasing shift towards lower dose, cleaner, and safer forms of tobacco. To put it bluntly, both NRTs mark a further stage in this longer-term sanitisation of smoking: the shift towards more and more controlled and individualised forms and usage of "tobacco," and the increasing use of nicotine as a means of self-control. 2) There's evidence—beyond this quote here—of smokers long employing NRTs as a means of continuing their use of tobacco (here as nicotine self-administration) not as a means of stopping (despite often good intentions from them and others). Also, conversely, recent studies suggest something like 40% of quit attempts are now made with e-cigarettes (ASH 2014).

In NRTs, pharmaceutical companies, albeit unwittingly, provided what tobacco companies could not: physically and socially safer sources of nicotine, and with it, a means to *keep* smoking. They also provided an important psychological and behavioural bridge between combustible tobacco and the e-cigarette. Of course, in tobacco control circles, NRTs were never intended for this purpose. Quite often, particularly in the context of stop smoking services, great lengths are gone to in order to ensure that end users view NRTs as therapies—with clear quit dates in mind; with the aim of gradually reducing the dose of (and, it is hoped, the user's dependence upon) nicotine. In a significant proportion of cases, this approach has the desired effect. In many others, it does not. The key point is that it is not the delivery mechanism that determines whether any particular device or substance constitutes a therapy or a drug, but, ultimately, *how these are understood and used by users*: the *social* uses of tobacco, and the *social* context of that use.

Policy makers draw neat categorical distinctions between NRTs (which are said to be "good" because they are understood to be a stop smoking device) and e-cigarettes (which are said to be "bad," because they are understood to be keep smoking devices—either by keeping a user using nicotine or, so the argument goes, through becoming a "gateway" or "bridge" to combustible tobacco), but these will not prevent users making their own decisions as to whether to use one or the other as a drug or a therapy. Some users will carry on using NRTs as a safer way to "smoke"; others will continue to use e-cigarettes in their attempts to quit, and vice versa. A further, step in the medicalisation of tobacco would involve e-cigarettes becoming appropriated as "therapies" (recent policy directives, such as the Tobacco Products Directive passed by the European Parliament in March 2014, suggest such a move is already underway). This would, of course, mean the development of increasingly tight controls over how e-cigarettes are sold, whom they are sold to, how they are packaged, how they are marketed, and how they are positioned to "consumers," or perhaps increasingly, "patients." It would mean that nicotine flavours would be outlawed, attractive packaging and user customisation too would need to be removed via legislation. If we continue with the possibility, in line with the longer-term shift towards sanitisation of tobacco use, e-cigarettes would likely come to resemble "inhalators," albeit delivering "vapour"—in highly regulated yields. Most importantly of all, it would be made clear to users that these devices were intended as cessation aids, and not as recreational products. But what would this achieve? Would the unintended consequences outweigh those, albeit highly laudable, ones that were intended?

To consider a parallel: ensuring codeine-based pain killers are available prescription only, not packaged attractively, and with clear dosing guidelines (together with all the usual warnings) does not stop them being used recreationally. Indeed, the misuse of prescription drugs in the US and, to a somewhat lesser extent, the UK, has become an increasingly large-scale problem in recent years. More importantly, if e-cigarettes are, so to speak, removed from the recreational space of tobacco use, might this in fact lead many users *back to* combustible sources? From the little that we know about the long-term effects of e-cigarettes, there are few who would question that they are much, much safer than their combustible counterparts: if e-cigarettes are dangerous in the longer-term, it is likely that NRTs will be too. E-cigarettes have the advantage, from a user's perspective, of mimicking some of the ritualistic aspects of smoking—the so-called hand-to-mouth pattern, and, of course, emulate the symbolism of smoking through vapour. They currently do not have the stigma of a therapy, and it is precisely because they are not sanitised, not associated with illness and recovery, and are perhaps even glamorous, that for some users, they are a far more appealing alternative to combustible tobacco than NRTs. In other words, some of the arguments about the glamorisation of e-cigarettes can be turned on their heads, at least in this key respect.

There is an even more radical possibility here, one that is perhaps unsayable in policy circles. But if it is the case that e-cigarettes are, on the whole, not that much more harmful than, say, drinking coffee, then might it be appropriate to accept that certain social groups should be permitted to "vape" without them having the intention of ever stopping? On what grounds would we reject recreational nicotine use if it no longer causes serious harm to the user? Moral grounds? Aesthetic grounds? The long-term history of the use of intoxicants would suggest that human beings are essentially a drug-using species. Might it then be more realistic to accept that there will always be a demand for the recreational consumption of tobacco (albeit as nicotine solution)?

Thus, to summarise I have argued that whether e-cigarettes are best conceived of as a cessation aid or a new means of using tobacco is not a matter that cannot be settled through policy classification, pharmacological distinctions, or through recourse to what happens at the level of brain chemistry, but through looking at the social uses and social contexts of that use. So once again, we need to understand the social dynamics of use, as well as the psychological/physiological/pharmacological ones. In particular, we need to consider the importance, once more, of changing social standards of behaviour.

The "Civilising" of Smoking

[Norbert] Elias, perhaps more than any other scholar, looked centrally at such changing behavioural standards in great depth. His most principal work, *On the Process of Civilisation,* is a complex, tome that is impossible to summarise in a few paragraphs in such a way as to do it any kind of justice. That said, his concept of "civilising processes" is indispensable to my present discussion. Elias traced long term changes in social standards of behaviour with a focus on the transition from the middle ages to modernity. He was centrally concerned with the tandem ascendancy of *modern societies* and the *modern self.* To oversimplify: his term, the "civilising process," refers to how changes in our psychological makeup are linked to changes in our social makeup.

Elias documents in meticulous detail a growing social pressure towards restraining and curbing our spontaneous impulses, what he calls the *social restraint towards self-restraint.* He argues that these social pressures follow from the growing monopolisation of violence and taxation by the state, and an increasing social imperative for people to attune themselves to ever more complex social networks. Civilising processes can be seen, for example, in long-term changes in our table manners. We come to develop all kinds of rules about the use of cutlery, about how we behave at the table, about the suppression of bodily functions, and so forth. These follow from the growing social pressure to curb spontaneous impulses and to display *refinement*: distinction from our supposed social inferiors, and how the latter displays become a growing source of *social capital*: how, within growing social circles, being able to handle yourself in company comes increasingly to matter more than how one handles oneself in, say, physical combat.

In the same way we might document a long-term "civilising" of tobacco use that is intimately bound up with these more general social processes. It can be seen, for example, in the shift away from the use of tobacco to lose control and escape normality (think, again, of the tobacco shaman falling into a death like trance), and the move towards the use of tobacco as an instrument of self-control that returns the user to "normality" (e.g. smoking to return one to "normal" by stimulation or relaxation). I have shown throughout this paper the significance of changing behavioural standards in driving these changes. In this process, I have argued, social dangers are as historically important as physical dangers. I have accordingly documented a long-term sanitisation of tobacco whereby tobacco has been "cleansed" of its smoke, and cleansed of disease.

For the moment at least, with e-cigarettes users can smoke in public without invading the air of others. There is no risk of fire, no risk of offence. The e-cigarette is surely the most "civilised" form of smoking thus far. E-cigarettes are non-invasive, (largely) non-offensive—a much "healthier," clinical, sanitised form of smoking. They are both physically and socially "safer" than any form of tobacco that has preceded them. They are "clean" in both an aesthetic and pharmacological sense. At the moment, users can "vape" in most public places (though this is changing rapidly, some countries such as Singapore and the UAE have already introduced a ban: e-cigarettes, it would seem, are guilty by association). Perhaps most interestingly, in the absence of any consensus regarding the physical dangers of smoking, debates have returned to the potential social dangers: might e-cigarettes serve as a "gateway drug," might they "renormalise" smoking, and more generally, might they be offensive to some "non-vapers." Seemingly without any clear evidential basis, the "gateway" hypothesis—that e-cigarettes are a gateway *to*, and not *from* (despite much evidence to the contrary), combustible tobacco—has come to hold considerable sway over the policy community. A timely case in point is the step changes introduced by the recent Tobacco Products Directive legislation mentioned earlier in this piece. The directive has recently been hailed as marking a great day for tobacco harm reduction. But viewed in the longer-term, viewed through the lens of the "civilising" of tobacco, this point is moot.

The directive effective continues the longer-term trend I have discussed throughout this piece—both the increasing sanitisation and regulation of smoking and the social pressure for the discursive reduction of tobacco to nicotine. Again, to labour the point somewhat, the policy is a response to *social pressures, not medical discovery*—indeed, the scientific case for regulating e-cigarettes is weak to say the least. Somewhat paradoxically, in responding to these social pressures, the policy might unintentionally play into the hands of large tobacco corporations who have seen their sales of combustible tobacco drop as much as 10% in tandem with the rise of e-cigarettes. As e-cigarettes become tightly regulated—soon requiring licensing, tightly controlled yield limits, etc.—who will be better placed than Big Tobacco to negotiate the rapidly increasing range and number of policy obstacles between the product and the marketplace? Who will have the resources, both financial and legal, to make the grade in policy terms? It is rather less likely that the many small producers and electronics start-ups that for the moment at least hold a significant share of the e-cigarette market will be able to compete. Big tobacco benefits not just by having an open road for potentially increasing their share of the e-cigarette market to the point of monopolisation, it also benefits through a potential resurgence in sales of combustible tobacco. If e-cigarettes are repositioned as a "stop smoking" device, smokers who wish to continue may well return to combustible tobacco, particularly if there is no longer a sufficient experiential equivalence between smoking and vaping as a consequence of tighter regulations. The threat posed to large pharmaceutical firms who produce NRTs also proportionally diminishes on two fronts—first as competition from e-cigarettes in the recreational space is reduced, and secondly because the somewhat perverse symbiosis between combustible tobacco and NRTs (the "drug" which underpins demand for "therapies"—which are treated as a different class of "thing") becomes restored.

This lens of civilising processes, then, is crucial to understanding the rise of e-cigarettes, and, more generally, to understanding the debates surrounding recent policy developments pertaining to these new devices.

11

Electronic Cigarettes: Good for Smokers, Bad for Teens

Janet Raloff

Janet Raloff has been a reporter at Science News for more than three decades, covering the environment, energy, science policy, and agriculture.

Not everyone was quite as convinced about electronic cigarettes and the perfect-enough solution they offered to the half-century- long health crisis of smoking. In 2014, a congressional report commissioned by a number of Democratic representatives and senators suggested otherwise, as Janet Raloff reported for Science News at the time. Raloff suggests that researchers had spent too much time in the lab and not enough time thinking of electronic cigarettes as products that would have to be sold in the marketplace and attempt to reach as many people as possible, arguing that the marketing of e-cigarettes is an under-explored but important aspect of the topic.

E lectronic-cigarette makers "are aggressively promoting their products using techniques and venues that appeal to youth," a new report finds. It concludes that the US government "should act quickly" to issue new laws.

The offices of 11 Democratic Senate and House members issued the report on April 14. In it, the writers argue that new laws should end the targeting of e-cigarette advertising at teens. The report

"E-Cigarette Makers Focus on Teens," by Janet Raloff, Society for Science and the Public, April 17, 2014. Used with permission.

also argues that there should be laws that ban the sale of these potentially addictive products to anyone under the age of 18.

E-cigarettes were developed as a way to help smokers stop using tobacco. But more and more people—especially teens—use these devices for fun and to look stylish. Scientists have begun to worry that teens might face harm from the nicotine and other substances in these products.

Nicotine is a natural chemical found in tobacco and other plants. It is responsible for the buzz smokers get from tobacco. It also is the chemical that makes tobacco addictive. Physicians worry that teens who practice vaping—the term for "smoking" electronic cigarettes—may develop an addiction to nicotine. And they note that nicotine can be toxic. Researchers have identified other toxic ingredients, as well, in some flavorings used in e-cigarettes.

But few scientists have taken a comprehensive look at how e-cigarette companies advertise their products. That's where the new congressional report fits in. It documents the practices of nine major companies making e-cigarettes.

Last September, the staff of these lawmakers contacted e-cigarette companies. They asked the companies to answer a list of questions. Those staff members also looked at packaging materials, product labels and company websites. And they asked what role the US Food and Drug Administration (FDA) can or should take to control youth access to e-cigarettes.

How Companies Can Target Teens

Based on what they learned, authors of the new report conclude that e-cigarettes should be regulated, much as tobacco products are now.

Federal law gives the FDA authority to regulate cigarettes and other tobacco products. Their sale, for instance, is banned for anyone under the age of 18. (Some states and towns are even more restrictive.) But these rules do not apply to e-cigarettes.

The FDA bans tobacco companies from sponsoring youth-oriented events and giveaways. Many e-cigarette companies now promote their products by sponsoring sporting, musical and other events that appeal to teens, the new survey finds. In addition, these companies sometimes give away free vaping products.

FDA rules ban the sale of tobacco laced with flavorings. This is intended to limit the appeal of tobacco products to kids. Yet the vapors inhaled from e-cigarettes come from a solution that can appeal to children. Flavors include fruits, candy, ice cream and more.

Federal rules say that cigarettes must be sold in face-to-face transactions. That's so the seller can confirm the age of whoever buys the product. No such limits apply to e-cigarettes.

Twenty-eight states (including New York, Illinois and California) have banned e-cigarette sales to minors. However, "industry self-regulation is the only way to prevent minors from buying e-cigarettes" in all other states, the report notes. Some vaping-product makers have asked stores to sell their products to adults only. Yet just three of eight of the surveyed companies say they actually check to see that stores do this.

Moreover, seven of the nine e-cigarette makers that were surveyed sell their products online. Such online sales are not legal for tobacco cigarettes. At least three companies that sell vaping products online told the congressional team they do not verify a buyer's age. Another three ask buyers if they are adults. But they also do nothing to confirm such statements are true.

Have you seen an e-cigarette ad? If not, you may very soon. The congressional report found that among companies that would share financial information, one had increased its spending on advertising for vaping products by 64 percent between 2012 and 2013. Another two companies said they tripled their spending last year.

A 1970 law bans cigarette ads on US radio and TV shows. The idea was to limit a child's access to such ads. This law does not apply to ads for vaping products. And indeed, seven of the nine companies surveyed said they were advertising on radio and TV. Those ads have run during the Super Bowl and Academy Awards, and on sports networks. It's certainly possible that kids are being exposed to this advertising, the congressional report concludes.

E-cigarette companies also reach out to potential new users via social media, including Facebook, Twitter, YouTube and Instagram. Some companies restrict comments or "likes" from minors. But others don't, the congressional study found—even though such tools are available to them.

Health Concerns Abound

The FDA requires labels warning of health risks on all cigarette packaging. Makers of vaping products do not have to carry such warnings. Still, eight of the nine surveyed companies say they do include some type of warning. Many include a statement saying that vaping products contain nicotine. The labels also state that the State of California says this chemical can cause birth defects or other reproductive harm. Such labels usually also warn that pregnant women should not vape.

Other warning labels say "this product does not treat, diagnose or cure any disease." Or they can state that nicotine may pose risks to people with heart disease, high blood pressure and diabetes.

Such warnings are not likely to scare off teens. The risks would appear largely for pregnant women and older people with chronic disease.

Yet there may be risks to teens, such as that from nicotine.

A 2014 report by the US Surgeon General summarized decades of research on nicotine effects. Those findings "suggest that exposure to nicotine in youth increases the risk of nicotine addiction," the new report notes. The report also pointed to data showing that "nicotine exposure during adolescence, a critical window for brain development, may have lasting adverse consequences."

How addictive is nicotine? The congressional report cites a 2007 study that found teens can show addictive behavior within two days of first smoking traditional cigarettes. E-cigarettes will likely have less nicotine than a tobacco product. But manufacturers do not have to report how much. So there is no way to know how much a teen might be exposed to through vaping.

The FDA notes that e-cigarettes have not been fully studied, so users "currently don't know the potential risks." The FDA doesn't even know to what chemicals a user might be exposed. One reason, the report notes: "E-cigarette manufacturers are currently not required to disclose to FDA a list of all ingredients." And they don't have to make available reports of harm linked to their products.

Several studies have shown some vaping products can contain substances that the FDA has already identified as being harmful or potentially harmful. Among them are heavy metals such as cadmium, nickel and lead. E-cigarette vapors also may include toxic chemicals such as formaldehyde, acetaldehyde, acrolein, toluene and nitrosamines.

Recommendations to Act

The new report recommends that the FDA move promptly to issue new rules that would prevent adolescent use of vaping products. Because research indicates nicotine can be especially harmful to children and teens, the report asks makers of vaping products to ban sales to minors, require face-to-face sales to adults and demand proof of any buyer's age.

Finally, the report recommends that the FDA require "strong, uniform labels" on e-cigarettes and vaping products warning of health risks that may be linked to them.

12

The FDA Takes the Hard Line

Iran Daily

*Iran Daily is the official daily newspaper of the government of Iran
and is run by the Islamic Republic News Agency, which is itself run
by the Iranian Ministry of Culture and Islamic Guidance.*

Iran Daily *reported in late 2018 that regulation was coming for
electronic cigarettes. The FDA would officially ban many of the
flavors used in the production of electronic cigarettes, a regulation
that would have a stronger effect in brick and mortar stores than on
the internet. Even more significant was the hardening of language,
calling the use of electronic cigarettes among teenagers an "epidemic."
There were now organizations unifying against the new cigarette
makers, and the FDA was hearing their appeals.*

The US Food and Drug Administration (FDA) next week will
issue a ban on the sale of fruit and candy flavored electronic
cigarettes in convenience stores and gas stations, an agency official
said, in a move to counter a surge in teenage use of e-cigarettes.

The ban means only tobacco, mint and menthol flavors can be
sold at these outlets, the agency official said, potentially dealing
a major blow to Juul Labs Inc., the San Francisco-based market
leader in vape devices, Reuters reported.

The FDA also will introduce stricter age-verification
requirements for online sales of e-cigarettes. The FDA's planned

restrictions, first reported by the *Washington Post* and confirmed to Reuters by the official, do not apply to vape shops or other specialty retail stores.

There has been mounting pressure for action after preliminary federal data showed teenage use had surged by more than 75 percent since last year, and the FDA has described it as an "epidemic."

"E-cigs have become an almost ubiquitous—and dangerous— trend among teens," FDA Commissioner Scott Gottlieb said in September.

"The disturbing and accelerating trajectory of use we're seeing in youth, and the resulting path to addiction, must end. It's simply not tolerable."

That growth has coincided with the rise of Juul, whose sales of vaping devices grew from 2.2 million in 2016 to 16.2 million devices last year, according to the US Centers for Disease Control and Prevention.

The agency threatened in September to ban Juul and four other leading e-cigarette products unless their makers took steps to prevent use by minors. The FDA gave Juul and four big tobacco companies 60 days to submit plans to curb underage use, a compliance period that is now ending.

The planned restrictions on flavors in convenience stores are likely to have the biggest impact on Juul, which sells nicotine liquid pods in flavors such as mango, mint, fruit and creme, previously called creme brulee.

The only other e-cigarette competitors sold at convenience stores are those marketed primarily by tobacco companies such as Altria Group, Inc., British American Tobacco p.l.c., Imperial Brands PLC and Japan Tobacco Inc.

Those products, sold under the MarkTen, blu, Vuse and Logic brands, have lost market share as Juul has risen to prominence over the last year, growing from 13.6 percent of the US e-cigarette market in early 2017 to nearly 75 percent now, according to a Wells Fargo analysis of Nielsen retail data.

E-cigarette products represent a small share of revenue for major tobacco companies, whereas Juul's business is built entirely on the vaping devices. Revenue from e-cigarette devices made up less than one percent of British American Tobacco's global revenue for the first six months of 2018, according to a company filing from July.

Altria last month announced it would stop selling its pod-based electronic cigarettes, generally smaller devices that use pre-filled nicotine liquid cartridges, in response to the FDA's concerns about teen usage. The company also said it would restrict flavors for its other e-cigarette products to tobacco, menthol and mint.

Representatives from Altria, British American Tobacco, Imperial Brands and Japan Tobacco did not respond to requests for comment. A Juul spokeswoman declined to comment.

The companies have previously said their products are intended for adult use and that they work to ensure retailers comply with the law.

Juul has previously said the company wants to be "part of the solution in keeping e-cigarettes out of the hands of young people" but that "appropriate flavors play an important role in helping adult smokers switch."

Meredith Berkman, a founder of Parents Against Vaping E-cigarettes, which seeks to curb underage use, said the agency's move was a "good first step," but added that "the final step should have happened yesterday."

"Why not do away with flavors altogether, why not do away with online sales altogether?" she said.

E-cigarettes have been a divisive topic in the public health community. Some focus on the potential for the products to shift lifelong smokers onto less harmful nicotine products, while others fear they risk drawing a new generation into nicotine addiction.

Last year the FDA, under Gottlieb, extended until 2022 a deadline for e-cigarette companies to comply with new federal rules on marketing and public health.

13

A Scientific Perspective on the Categorization of E-Cigarettes

Raphaela Putzhammer, Christian Doppler, Thomas Jakschitz, Katharina Heinz, Juliane Förste, Katarina Danzl, Barbara Messner, and David Bernhard

Raphaela Putzhammer, Christian Doppler, Katharina Heinz, Juliane Förste, Katarina Danzl and David Bernhard are affiliated with the Cardiac Surgery Research Laboratory at the Medical University of Innsbruck in Austria. Thomas Jakschitz is affiliated with the Austrian Drug Screening Institute GmbH. Barbara Messner is affiliated with the Cardiac Surgery Research Laboratory at the Medical University of Vienna, Austria.

The excerpted study below presents a technical way to think about electronic cigarettes as products that work in a specific way and need to be categorized in order to, ultimately, be considered seriously. Its invention at the turn of the millennium makes the electronic cigarette not just another new product, but one of the first products to be designed and marketed to new, internet-savvy audiences, and its technical specifications have a lot to tell us about how that kind of marketing materializes in the products. The toxicology information, in kind, presents us with the cold and vital data needed to view electronic cigarettes as items themselves, generators of their own causes and health effects.

Raphaela Putzhammer, Christian Doppler, Thomas Jakschitz, Katharina Heinz, Juliane Förste, Katarina Danzl, Barbara Messner, and David Bernhard, "Vapours of US and EU Market Leader Electronic Cigarette Brands and Liquids Are Cytotoxic for Human Vascular Endothelial Cells," 11(6) (June 28, 2016). Available at: https://www.ncbi.nlm.nih.gov/pmc/articles/PMC4924852/. This article is brought to you for free and open access by PLoS ONE courtesy of Public Library of Science.

The present study was conducted to provide toxicological data on e-cigarette vapours of different e-cigarette brands and liquids from systems viewed as leaders in the e-cigarette market and to compare e-cigarette vapour toxicity to the toxicity of conventional strong high-nicotine cigarette smoke. Using an adapted version of a previously constructed cigarette smoke constituent sampling device, we collected the hydrophilic fraction of e-cigarette vapour and exposed human umbilical vein endothelial cells (HUVECs) to the mixture of compounds present in the vapour of 4 different single-use e-cigarettes, 6 different liquid vapours produced by the same refillable e-cigarette, and one e-cigarette with an exchangeable liquid cartridge. After incubation of cells with various concentrations and for various periods of time we analysed cell death induction, proliferation rates, the occurrence of intra-cellular reactive oxygen species, cell morphology, and we also measured e-cigarette heating coil temperatures. Overall, conventional cigarette smoke extract showed the most severe impact on endothelial cells. However, some e-cigarette vapour extracts showed high cytotoxicity, inhibition of cell proliferation, and alterations in cell morphology, which were comparable to conventional high-nicotine cigarettes. The vapours generated from different liquids using the same e-cigarette show substantial differences, pointing to the liquids as an important source for toxicity. E-cigarette vapour-mediated induction of oxidative stress was significant in one out of the 11 analysed vapours. There is a high variability in the acute cytotoxicity of e-cigarette vapours depending on the liquid and on the e-cigarettes used. Some products showed toxic effects close to a conventional high-nicotine cigarette. Liquid nicotine, menthol content, and the formation of acute intracellular reactive oxygen species do not seem to be the central elements in e-cigarette vapour toxicity.

Introduction

The e-cigarette is generally promoted as "the healthier alternative" referring to a less harmful alternative to conventional cigarettes. The biggest market for e-cigarettes and liquids is the internet. By the end of 2014, 466 e-cigarette brands and 7764 types of e-liquid existed. While international and national health legislation and regulation for e-cigarettes are still being developed, it has become clear that no reliable, objective and standardised systems are available yet that can test for e-cigarette liquid and vapour toxicity.

[...]

The second major element in e-cigarette vapour toxicity is the composition of liquids. Currently available liquid bases contain water, glycerol, propylene glycol, or mixtures of these compounds. Particularly, when heating the liquid base itself or the aroma compounds added within, new compounds may form, e.g. propylene oxide (from propylene glycol) or acrolein (from glycerol), which have well documented carcinogenic properties. Many e-cigarette liquids contain nicotine and several liquids which are actually sold as "nicotine-free" liquids have, in fact, been found to contain nicotine. Even though the toxicity associated with the nicotine concentrations delivered through most e-cigarettes may not be substantial, nicotine remains one of the most addictive substances known. The dosages of nicotine applied to the consumer when using e-cigarettes are unclear, not only because of ambiguous declaration of content by some producers/traders, but also because the vaporization process varies significantly between e-cigarette brands. Importantly, a standardised method for indicating nicotine concentration is lacking, resulting in incomparable information ranging from concentrations (mg/ml), total amount, to low-middle-high scales.

Similar to conventional cigarettes, e-cigarette liquids contain artificial flavouring. Some of these flavours are already known to be toxic. The effects of flavouring compounds, when modified by heating and/or interaction with other agents contained in the liquid is mainly unknown. The discovery of Tandalafil (virility promoting agent) and Rimonabant (appetite suppressant) in e-cigarette liquids may indicate the urgent need for a better protection of consumers through quality control guidelines by national and international health institutions.

The third component in e-cigarette vapour toxicity is the vaporizer itself and materials used for constructing the hardware which come in physical contact with the user or the liquid. As an example, and probably as a central element in "hardware-based toxicity," various metals have been shown to be released from the wire used as the heating element of the vaporizer. This wire is in permanent and direct contact with the e-liquid and, upon use, generates the vapour that is inhaled by the e-cigarette user. Metals such as aluminium, chromium, copper, lead, nickel, silver, and tin, have been found in e-cigarette vapour and their relevance has previously been discussed in conventional cigarette smoke.

To date potential adverse effects of e-cigarette use on human health are not well defined as the products are still new and technology is changing rapidly. Particularly long term consequences of e-cigarette use are unclear.

[...]

Materials and Methods

Materials

Based on an in-depth internet investigation, we selected e-cigarettes according to the following criteria: i) availability of a broad spectrum of different products (disposable e-cigarettes, e-cigarettes with a cartridge and e-cigarettes with refillable liquids), ii) products viewed as leaders in the European and USA e-cigarette market, iii) most popular flavours (tobacco, menthol, fruit flavours), and iv) liquids without as well as with various concentrations of nicotine. All liquids tested were vaporized with the identical vaporizer system. The high-nicotine conventional strength cigarette, as a reference, as well as the technology of smoke extract preparation has been reported previously.

Cigarette Smoke and E-Cigarette Vapour Extract Generation

Cigarette smoke and e-cigarette vapour extracts were generated as previously described. For e-cigarettes that required the vaporizer to be switched on manually, the operator of the smoke/vapour-generating machine pressed the "on button" on the e-cigarette 1 second prior to each of the automatic "drag phases" (which lasts for 2 seconds) of the machine and activated the e-cigarette until the end of the drag phase. For all cigarettes and liquids tested, the extracts were generated in the same manner; i.e. 20 cycles of 2 seconds dragging on the cigarette (35 ml / 2 seconds), followed by a 28 seconds pause. All e-cigarettes were fixed to a horizontal position while vapour was being generated. Importantly, all devices/tubes etc. in contact with smoke or vapour were exchanged between the extract preparation steps of each product and cleaned prior to re-use by intensive washing with ethanol (ultrapure) and water (ultrapure). The generation of vapour from identical amounts of liquid for all products tested was controlled by weighing the liquid cartridge (refill products) or the entire e-cigarette (single use devices) prior and after extract generation. Per generation of one extract (i.e. 20 puffs) a total of 88 +/- 5 mg of liquid was vaporized.

[...]

Exposure of Cells to Smoke and Vapour Extracts

Prior to exposure of cells to smoke or vapour extracts, cells were trypsinized, washed, counted and seeded into 6 well plates (300,000 cells per well for 1 and 24 hour exposures, and 150,000 cells per well for 48 hour exposures), and allowed to adhere overnight. Prior to each experiment cell culture medium was replaced with fresh medium. For each experiment smoke and vapour extracts were freshly generated, filtered through a 0.2 µm filter, and applied directly to the cells by addition of the extracts to the culture plates to achieve the different % of extracts indicated. The extract concentrations chosen are based on our previous studies on conventional cigarettes with the assumption that e-cigarette consumers inhale a comparable volume of vapour to the volume of smoke inhaled by a conventional smoker (35 ml / puff, 10 puffs per cigarette). The system was previously adjusted to generate nicotine concentrations in the smoke extract which were similar to nicotine concentrations found in the blood of smokers. As e-cigarette liquids do not contain a defined set of compounds which may allow for a standardisation, different extracts were compared by analysing the biological effects of equal amounts of the different vapour extracts. One hundred % extract corresponds to 20 times 35 ml of vapour drawn through 8 ml of culture medium.

Quantification of Cell Death

For detection and quantification of cell death, forward/sideward light scattering analysis and annexin V (AxV) / propidium iodide (PI)-staining were used as described. AxV / PI-staining allows for the discrimination between intact viable cells (AxV-negative / PI-negative), apoptotic (AxV-positive / PI-negative) and necrotic cells (AxV-positive / PI-positive). After incubation of cells with e-cigarette extracts and cigarette smoke extracts for 24 hours (data not shown) and 48 hours, cells were stained and analysed using a FACS Calibur (BD, Vienna, Austria). The distribution of cells into the above groups was assessed; data are expressed as mean values and cells were categorized into either viable cells (AxV / PI-double negative cells) or dead cells (total cells minus AxV / PI double negative cells). The rationale for not differentiating between apoptotic and necrotic cells was that almost exclusively necrotic cell death was observed.

[...]

Results

Five out of Eleven E-Cigarette Vapours
Analysed Show Acute Cytotoxicity

In order to reveal potential cytotoxic effects of e-cigarette vapours from various liquids, we generated e-cigarette vapour extracts and exposed HUVECs to these vapours for 48 hours. These analyses showed that 5 (B/1, Cre2, Cre4, Cre5, Cre6) out of 11 e-cigarettes or e-liquids tested showed a statistically significant increase in cell death, two of them already at a lower concentration of 8% (Cre4 and Cre6). Another major finding of these analyses was that 3 (Cre2, Cre 5, Cre6) out of 6 liquids which were vaporized using the same system showed dramatic cytotoxic effects, and reached toxicity close to conventional strength high-nicotine cigarettes. Of interest is also that 2 (Cre5 and Cre6) of these 3 highly toxic liquids did not contain nicotine, but were flavoured with berry or herbal constituents. In this study also data for 24 hours were obtained.

Five out of Eleven E-Cigarette Vapours Reduce the Proliferation of Endothelial Cells

The analyses of the proliferation inhibiting activity of e-cigarette vapour extracts revealed that 5 (A/2, Cre2, Cre3, Cre5, Cre6) out of 11 e-cigarettes or e-liquids tested showed a statistically significant reduction of cell proliferation. Importantly, toxicity of chemicals is a major reason for reduced proliferation of cells, and the reduction of proliferation—in case of toxicity—is a more sensitive parameter compared to cell death, as it already occurs at lower concentrations of those chemicals. In case of the 11 e-cigarette vapours analysed, the indication of toxicity as the source for reduced proliferation can well be observed as the three extracts with the highest cytotoxicity (Cre2, Cre5, and Cre6, see above) are also the extracts which most potently inhibited cell proliferation. Interestingly, although no significant increase in cell death extent was observable after incubation with Cre3 e-liquid, the proliferation of HUVECs is significantly reduced by this liquid. In this study also data for 24 hours were obtained.

[...]

Toxic E-Cigarette Vapour Extracts Cause Morphological Alterations in Endothelial Cells Similar to Conventional Cigarette Smoke Extracts

In a previous study we could show that conventional cigarette smoke extracts disrupt the vascular endothelial barrier function by breaking up cell-cell contacts and by inducting a collapse of the microtubule system, both leading to a detachment like phenotype. In order to analyse the impact of e-cigarette vapour extracts on endothelial shape, cells were treated with vapour extracts of Cre2, Cre5, and Cre6, similar to conventional cigarette smoke extracts, also e-cigarette vapours cause significant morphological alterations in endothelial cells and disrupt the functional endothelial monolayer, represented by the controls (0%). Whereas high concentrations of vapour extracts are toxic to endothelial cells, which leads to death induced detachment of cells, non- or slightly toxic concentrations (8%) also cause morphological changes which will certainly contribute to disease-induction by e-cigarette vapours.

[...]

Discussion

Effects of E-Cigarette Vapour on Cells and Tissues

An increasing number of valid and excellent scientific publications are available on the role and dangers of e-cigarette use, as a potential tool for cessation, and also in the field of toxicity. Until now there are important, yet few, studies available which analysed e-cigarette vapour toxicity, the majority of which support the view that e-cigarette vapour is toxic. Previous studies have revealed e-cigarette-mediated alterations in glucose and lipid metabolism, also by liquids free of nicotine, an impact on the transcriptome of bronchial epithelial cells involving alterations in glycerophospholipid metabolism, cytotoxicity and pro-inflammatory signalling due to flavour-derived reactive oxygen species inhalation in the lung, and cell death and pro-inflammatory cytokine release by lung and skin derived cell lines. Oxidative stress and inflammation are processes which are also thought to be central for the cytotoxicity of conventional cigarette smoke. E-cigarette vapour specific processes and cytotoxicity are not well understood. Clearly this lack of information is due to the fact that e-cigarette toxicity research is a young field of research, but is also influenced by the fact that different liquids contain different toxic compounds with differing cytotoxic profiles—a view that is supported by studies by Lerner et al. and Behar et al. and the present study. It was the goal of the present study to obtain data on the cytotoxic and proliferation-inhibiting effects of e-cigarette vapours from different brands and liquids—all of which are currently considered as market leader products. By analysing cell death, proliferation, the formation of reactive oxygen species, by morphological analyses of HUVECs, and by choosing different sets of e-cigarettes and liquids (e.g. with and without nicotine, menthol etc.), this study allows new insights on potential pathogenic mechanisms and the role of some ingredients—certainly with limitations. Given the fact that there are currently almost 10,000 different liquids available, this study (analysing 11 different vapours) is limited in its validity. Nevertheless—due to the choice of market leader products—basic results are of relevance.

Central Findings of the Present Study

1. The highest toxicity of all liquid extracts tested is found in liquid-refill devices. Of great importance is the observation that toxicity and inhibition of proliferation was highly dependent on the type of liquid used.

2. Disposable products seem to be less toxic. Importantly, the "satisfactory feeling" of the user, when consuming e-cigarette vapour, was not assessed in this study. When adapting results from conventional cigarettes and conventional smokers, where it was shown that smoking behaviour is changed unconsciously due to the use of "light cigarettes," similar subconscious traits may occur in e-cigarette use. The analysis of toxicity and compounds in e-cigarette vapour under different conditions of e-cigarette use shall be a central part of future studies.

3. Despite the fact that nicotine is the central reason for tobacco/cigarette (e-cigarette) dependence, vapour-extract toxicity does not correlate with nicotine content. Other

studies suggest however, that nicotine may alter cellular responses and activate additional, potentially pathologically relevant signalling pathways. In the present study no correlation between the menthol content and toxicity was observed. Importantly, these statements are based on information provided by the manufacturers, and since the majority of liquid ingredients are not disclosed by companies, and not known by the authors, these statements need to be verified by chemical analyses of liquids by unbiased scientists.

4. In our study, particularly herbal flavours seem to contain highly toxic compounds; plant extracts contain a huge number of different compounds, the nature of the toxicity-relevant compounds is unknown. Previously, similar effects were observed with cinnamon flavoured liquids.

5. The formation of intracellular reactive oxygen species by e-cigarette vapour extracts was not correlated to their toxicity in our study. Lerner et al. showed however, that reactive oxygen species and copper (which catalyses the formation of reactive oxygen species) may contribute to e-cigarette smoke-mediated inflammation in the lung. Despite the fact that the role of reactive oxygen species is not clear, cell type specific processes may be at play. Based on our results, one would speculate that toxicity mechanisms of some e-cigarette vapours in endothelial cells may differ from those of conventional cigarettes, where reactive oxygen species are central for disease induction.

6. The analysis of vaporizer heating coil temperatures during use, and the optical characteristics of e-liquid which remains in the cartridge, suggest that temperatures that are applied to liquids in e-cigarettes may be significantly higher than proposed by manufacturers, and that some liquids upon use undergo chemical modifications (aging/oxidation processes, similar to the Maillard reaction), and tend to precipitation or may even facilitate microbial growth.

Conclusions

Given the fact that at least one out of 11 products tested herein was close to the toxicity of a conventional strength high-nicotine cigarette in the absence of high levels of reactive oxygen species, e-cigarette vapour-mediated patho-mechanisms and e-liquid (vapour) contained compounds are likely to impact human health in a way that differs from conventional cigarettes. This hypothesis is of particular interest regarding long term health effects of e-cigarette use.

Generally, e-cigarette vapour constituents affect cell viability, proliferation, morphology, metabolism, and state of inflammatory activation. All these alterations show that chemicals found in e-cigarette vapour influence cells in a fundamental way and broad manner. Based on the current knowledge, a precise definition of diseases that may be caused by chronic exposure to e-cigarette vapours in humans is not possible, but current data allow stating that e-cigarette use is indeed harmful.

14

Harm Minimization, Vaping, and the Need for Proactive Policy

David B. Abrams, Allison M. Glasser, Jennifer L. Pearson, Andrea C. Villanti, Lauren K. Collins, and Raymond S. Niaura

David B. Abrams and Raymond S. Niaura are affiliated with the College of Global Public Health at New York University. Allison M. Glasser and Lauren K. Collins are affiliated with the Schroeder Institute for Tobacco Research and Policy Studies' Truth Initiative. Jennifer L. Pearson is affiliated with the School of Community Health Sciences at the University of Nevada—Reno. Andrea C. Villanti is affiliated with the Vermont Center on Behavior and Health at the University of Vermont.

In the research presented in this viewpoint, the study's authors suggest that e-cigarettes and other alternative nicotine delivery systems (ANDS) are essential to disrupt cigarette smoking and decouple nicotine from inhaled smoke, which is the lethal aspect of cigarette smoking. The opportunity to minimize harm and save lives makes pro-ANDS policy essential, according to the authors. Eliminating nicotine use may be impossible, so reframing how society uses nicotine through the use of e-cigarettes and ANDS is the best way forward.

"Harm Minimization and Tobacco Control: Reframing Societal Views of Nicotine Use to Rapidly Save Lives," by David B. Abrams, Allison M. Glasser, Jennifer L. Pearson, Andrea C. Villanti, Lauren K. Collins, and Raymond S. Niaura, *Annual Review of Public Health*, January 11, 2018. https://www.annualreviews.org/doi/pdf/10.1146/annurev-publhealth-040617-013849. Licensed under CC BY-SA 4.0 International.

The fiftieth-anniversary US Surgeon General's Report, in 2014, concluded, "The burden of death and disease from tobacco use in the US is overwhelmingly caused by cigarette and other combusted tobacco products; rapid elimination of their use will dramatically reduce this burden." Globally, smoking-caused annual deaths will rise to 8 million by 2030 if current trends continue. It is imperative to find additional ways to accelerate the decline in smoking because, if nothing changes, a billion lives will be lost prematurely by 2100. Despite declines over the last 50 years, ~520,000 Americans annually die prematurely from smoking-related causes. The Surgeon General stated, "The current rate of progress in tobacco control is not fast enough. More needs to be done." The US Food and Drug Administration (FDA) commissioner endorsed the need for striking an appropriate balance between regulation and encouragement of the development of innovative nicotine or noncombustible tobacco products that are less dangerous than cigarettes. It is past time to add new and even radical approaches.

The term alternative nicotine delivery systems (ANDS) encompasses a diverse class of noncombustible smokeless tobacco products or nicotine-containing products, primarily exemplified by e-cigarettes that are vaped not smoked. ANDS raise fundamental questions for society: Could ANDS be leveraged to effectively compete with cigarettes, eventually making smoking obsolete sooner than would otherwise be possible? Can many types of ANDS, when decoupled from deadly toxins in combusted tobacco smoke, be accepted by the public and by its health, regulatory, and advocacy bodies as an extraordinary opportunity to save lives rather than as a threat to the success of past tobacco control efforts? These questions are contentious, and their answers are complicated. Addressing opportunities for ANDS requires reexamination of the role that nicotine plays in sustaining smoking and the role that nicotine can play in reducing smoking when delivered in a safer, yet appealing manner. In a major shift in FDA policy following the FDA Commissioner's announcement, a new national comprehensive nicotine management strategy was proposed: "The agency's new tobacco strategy has two primary parts: reducing the addictiveness of combustible cigarettes while recognizing and clarifying the role that potentially less harmful tobacco products could play in improving public health ... Reducing cigarettes' addictiveness could help users quit more easily and help keep those who are experimenting—young people, in particular—from becoming regular smokers ... The availability of potentially less harmful tobacco products could reduce risk while delivering satisfying levels of nicotine for adults who still need or want it."

Reexamination of nicotine's role in society requires reconsidering the harm minimization perspective within tobacco control. The primary goal of harm minimization is to prevent the use of nicotine-containing products among nonusers, while pragmatically acknowledging that less harmful noncombusted nicotine products either with tobacco (e.g., snus) or without tobacco (e.g., e-cigarettes) can dramatically reduce risk compared with smoking combusted products. Harm minimization is wholly consistent with tobacco control goals to prevent any use by underage youth and encourage complete smoking cessation in both youth and adults and is responsive to the Surgeon General's admonition that more must be done to eliminate smoking tobacco.

We suggest a science-based reframing of nicotine use to inform current and future US and global tobacco control strategies. We use e-cigarettes as exemplars of ANDS, but newer types of ANDS products (e.g., that heat and do not burn tobacco) and accumulating scientific evidence will require continued discussions about managing nicotine's changing role in society. At times, our use of the term ANDS may also encompass classes of substantially less harmful noncombustible modes of nicotine delivery [i.e., medicinal nicotine replacement therapy (NRT), low nitrosamine Swedish snus, any smokeless tobacco, e-cigarettes].

The changing landscape of innovative reduced-harm products calls for a refocusing of tobacco control strategies, concentrating specifically on smoking control. Some traditional strategies will continue to be effective, whereas others may become ineffective or possibly iatrogenic if they slow rather than speed the demise of smoking. Herein, we integrate science and policy analysis to address the critical questions that underpin public health practice, policy, regulation, advocacy, and communication on nicotine-containing products.

Reframing Tobacco Control and Nicotine Use

Decades of tobacco control interventions (e.g., age purchasing restrictions, taxation, media campaigns, cessation services) have significantly decreased smoking prevalence in the United States. The 2009 Tobacco Control Act (TCA) and the newly promulgated nicotine management strategy complement tobacco control efforts by giving the FDA statutory authority to regulate tobacco and ANDS products. The TCA includes a public health standard that requires regulators to consider the net impact of tobacco products on the population as a whole, including smokers and nonsmokers. Adding to the FDA's prior role [via the Center for Drug Evaluation Research (CDER)] of approving medicinal products (e.g., NRT) for smoking cessation, the FDA established the Center for Tobacco Products (CTP) to regulate the manufacture, distribution, and marketing of tobacco and emerging nicotine products for consumer use (i.e., recreational rather than medicinal).

Whereas the CTP's authorities seek to protect the public from products that could harm public health, the CTP can also promote public health by supporting products (e.g., using product standards) and encouraging behaviors that maximize net population benefits by displacing smoking. Public education by the CTP can change behavior by informing smokers about the harms of different classes of refined nicotine products, compared with both smoking (relative risk) and no use (absolute risk).

Both the emergence of ANDS products and the TCA provide an opportunity to enrich tobacco control with a harm minimization framework. The following sections use e-cigarettes as the main case example of the individual health and the population health potential of selected harm minimization strategies.

Decoupling Nicotine from Inhaled Smoke for Harm Minimization

The logic of smoking harm minimization is simple and compelling. As Michael Russell, a pioneer in the field, put it, "People smoke for nicotine but they die from the tar." In getting the nicotine they seek, smokers are exposed to enormous harm, including from cardiovascular disease, cancer, and pulmonary diseases, due to the inhalation of toxic smoke from tobacco combustion products. For most smokers, there is little evidence that nicotine itself causes any of these classes of disease when decoupled from smoke. Although nicotine use poses some risk for vulnerable groups (e.g., with cardiovascular disease or during pregnancy), this risk is substantially lower than the risk posed by continuing to smoke cigarettes. Nicotine itself does not appear to cause cancer, even in former smokers who use low nitrosamine snus for decades. Evidence also indicates that nicotine itself is relatively safe when obtained from FDA-approved NRT, which is widely used for smoking cessation. E-cigarettes deliver nicotine without any tobacco in aerosol form (known as vapor). Smokers switching to vaping have experienced improved lung capacity and less frequent asthma events. At the doses that smokers experience, nicotine itself carries minimal harm. Thus, if smokers could be shifted from smoking to consuming clean nicotine (i.e., without smoke), many lives would be saved. The safest course is to stop smoking or, better, never to start. But a harm minimization approach recognizes that demanding absolute perfection is often counterproductive and that, when a harmful behavior cannot be eliminated, it is necessary to reduce its adverse health consequences. For those who are smoking and are unwilling or unable to quit nicotine use, moving to cleaner ANDS, including e-cigarettes, NRTs, or low nitrosamine snus, would reduce harm relative to smoking.

[...]

Systems Integration: Optimizing Population Benefits Over Harms

Population net exposure to harmful toxicants depends on the actual patterns and prevalence of product use, which vary along the continuum of harm.

Individuals begin in the noncurrent use state (a variant of never use) and can either remain in that state or transition to current exclusive use of cigarettes or ANDS or to dual use. Once in a current use state, individuals can maintain use, transition to one of two alternative states, or cease use of both products. Former users may also maintain no use or relapse to current exclusive or dual use. The CTP's public health standard implies an integrated consideration of product harms and benefits at the individual and population levels (including likelihoods of initiation and cessation). Population health could be improved by changes in nicotine-containing product use that result in transitions to less harmful use states. These changes include limiting movement from noncurrent use (i.e., preventing initiation of any nicotine product use by nonusers) and increasing movement away from cigarette use (perhaps via dual use) to exclusive use of less harmful ANDS and/or increased transition to former use and reduced relapse to smoking.

Each tobacco control strategy (e.g., taxes, media campaigns, treatment availability, accurate consumer knowledge of relative harms, regulations) will influence the flows from one state to another. Prevention of youth initiation and support for cessation will keep noncurrent and former users from starting or relapsing. Harm minimization strategies facilitate movement away from smoking regulating and managing products according to their relative harms. Outcomes are determined empirically by estimating the prevalence rates within states and the transition rates between states based on population surveillance. Simulation modeling of the effects of policies and regulations on transition rates can indicate where harms might exceed benefits, given different scenarios of product use.

Three examples of these approaches could be (*a*) imposing a differential tax on nicotine-containing products that is proportional to their degree of harm, with less harmful products being minimally taxed and all combusted products being very highly taxed; (*b*) reducing the addiction liability of combusted tobacco via nicotine reduction while ensuring adequate and satisfying nicotine delivery in ANDS; and (*c*) reducing the appeal of smoking by banning menthol and other flavors in smoked products but not in ANDS. Making combusted tobacco more expensive and less appealing while making ANDS more appealing, less harmful, and less costly are consistent with fully embracing harm minimization to speed users away from smoking as the primary end goal.

[...]

Policy Implications

The harm minimization approach yields clear implications for tobacco control policies, which demands a reorientation of these policies starting with a return to their harm minimization roots. A core harm minimization principle is that policy, regulation, and advocacy be science based and proportional to the degree of product harm, with the most restrictive strategies applying to the most harmful products.

Reaffirming Harm Minimization in Tobacco Control
Harm minimization was an accepted strategy at the beginning of tobacco control efforts in the 1960s. It was and still is implicit in tobacco control support for CDER-approved over-the-counter

use of NRT as a safe nicotine product. Public health advocates are now often skeptical of reduced harm products because of mistrust of the tobacco industry and commercial entities more generally, given the experience of the highly misleading promotion of low-tar "light" cigarettes that were not, in fact, reduced-harm products. This skepticism has generalized, negating all harm minimization strategies and data, including the well-documented successful Swedish experience with snus. Smokeless tobacco is still viewed by the World Health Organization and most countries as "not a safe alternative to smoking" even if it is much less harmful, and e-cigarettes are also being banned in many countries.

Harm minimization approaches have often been resisted in many areas of risky behavior because of fears of unintended harmful consequences. But when carefully implemented, these approaches have dramatically reduced harm at the individual and population levels [e.g., condom use and needle-exchange programs for HIV prevention].

Industry Considerations

In tobacco control, there is understandable trepidation in supporting alternatives that may risk undermining 50 years of tobacco control efforts, given past tobacco industry behavior. While holding the traditional tobacco industry and the newer ANDS industries strictly accountable, if, out of an abundance of caution, tobacco control strategies fail to fully embrace movement to less harmful products (or actively discourage such movement), the result could be detrimental for smokers who are unable to quit or who do not wish to quit nicotine use completely. A key question is whether the combination of technological advances (i.e., ANDS) and regulation can align makers of safer nicotine-containing products with public health advocates to eliminate combusted tobacco as a defective and unacceptable product for human use.

Public Education and Communication

Accurate public information is a crucial part of tobacco control policy. The positive impact of e-cigarettes may have been slowed by exaggerated claims of their harms and the harms of nicotine in general. Only 5.3% of Americans correctly believe that e-cigarettes are "much less harmful" than cigarettes, 37% believe they are the same or worse than smoking, and 34% don't know. Misperceptions of the harms of nicotine and e-cigarettes have recently increased, undermining their full potential to displace smoking. A misinformed public lacks the information required to take health-protective action. Accurate public education is needed to counteract misperceptions of harm from nicotine and ANDS, to communicate the continuum of risk related to the use of different tobacco and ANDS products, and to emphasize the importance of smoking cessation. ANDS should always be compared with smoked tobacco products (relative harms), and the mistaken public beliefs that nicotine is the cause of disease risk and cancer, rather than the smoke from combustion, must be dispelled. Fears that nicotine causes cancer discourages use of FDA-approved NRTs as well as e-cigarettes and other ANDS as viable ways to stop smoking cigarettes.

Conclusions

Harm minimization is a pragmatic approach that can complement proven current tobacco control efforts of prevention and cessation. Its primary goal is to move the whole population of smokers of toxic combusted tobacco products to exclusive use of much safer products as quickly and as early as possible in their individual smoking careers. If prudently regulated, e-cigarettes and Swedish snus provide a great opportunity to disrupt the US and global smoking-related disease pandemic and offer a proof-of-principle for the potential role of further innovations in ANDS in improving public health. This opportunity depends on encouraging increased technological innovation and finding the appropriate balance between product safety, consumer appeal, and regulations targeted specifically to decrease the use of conventional, combusted tobacco products.

Regulation, policy, practice, and advocacy for harm minimization approaches have the potential to realign market forces and economic incentives for those willing to responsibly manufacture and market much less harmful ANDS products to adult consumers. Even if the risk of harm to some youth who otherwise would not have smoked is marginally increased, such risks must be weighed against the substantial and immediate benefits of displacing smoking with safer nicotine products among both youth and adults. Under all but the most implausible scenarios, population simulation modeling estimates millions of life years saved by employing the principles of harm minimization and switching smokers to safer ANDS products. Replacement of most cigarette use by e-cigarette use over a 10-year period yields up to 6.6 million fewer premature deaths with 86.7 million fewer life years lost. America and the world need a candid smoking control champion—a figure like C. Everett Koop, Surgeon General during the first eight years of the AIDS epidemic—to get out the latest accurate information about reduced harm ANDS products that could save millions of smokers' lives. Ethics and integrity in responsibly interpreting the scientific evidence with rigor, and with common sense, demand it.

Organizations to Contact

The editors have compiled the following list of organizations concerned with the issues debated in this book. The descriptions are derived from materials provided by the organizations. All have publications or information available for interested readers. The list was compiled on the date of publication of the present volume; the information provided here may change. Be aware that many organizations take several weeks or longer to respond to inquiries, so allow as much time as possible.

American Vaping Association
70 Hemlock St.
Stratford, CT 06615
phone: (609) 947-8059
email: board@vaping.info
website: vaping.org

A nonprofit industry group sponsored by electronic cigarette companies and distributors VaporBeast and Pure Cigs, the American Vaping Association is the primary group advocating on behalf of small- and medium-sized businesses in the marketplace.

Anti-Vaping Online Information Dissemination (AVOID)
1175 Peachtree St. NE, Ste. 1600
Atlanta, GA 30361
phone: (404) 968-8008
email: publicaffairs@kdhrc.com
website: kdhrc.com/programs/avoid-anti-vaping-online-information-dissemination/

Anti-Vaping Online Information Dissemination, or AVOID, is an arm of KDH Research & Communication that is working to design anti-electronic cigarette educational materials aimed at 12-16 years olds.

Consumer Advocates for Smoke-Free Alternatives Association
CASAA
PO Box 2991
Plattsburgh, NY 12901
phone: (202) 241-9117
email: board@casaa.org
website: www.casaa.org

A nonprofit consumer organization with over 200,000 members dedicated to increasing recognition that smoke-free nicotine-containing products are inherently far less dangerous than smoking.

E-Cigarettes & the Fight Against Tobacco
1250 Connecticut Ave. NW, 7th Fl.
Washington, DC 20036
phone: (202) 659-4310
email: info@ash.org
website: www.ash.org

E-Cigarettes & the Fight Against Tobacco is a project by Action on Smoking & Health, a nonprofit based in Washington, DC, that works on lobbying against the tobacco industry, which also means against the electronic cigarette industry.

Smoke Free Alternatives Trade Association
1155 F St. NW, Ste. 1050
Washington, DC 20004
phone: (202) 251-1661
email: info@sfata.org
website: www.sfata.org

A DC-based electronic cigarette lobbying group, the Smoke Free Alternatives Trade Association largely aims to garner approval the greater public and is the host of the annual "Save the Vape" conference.

Tobacco Vapor Electronic Cigarette Association
1005 Union Center Dr., Ste. F
Alpharetta, GA 30004
phone: 1 (888) 99-TVECA
email: info@tveca.com
website: www.tveca.com

An international nonprofit split between the US and the European Union, the organization advocates on behalf of electronic cigarette makers around the world, promoting the widespread use of e-cigarettes.

UK Vaping Industry Association
34 Smith Square
London SW1P 3HL
United Kingdom
phone: 011 0203 267 0074
email: ukvia@jbp.co.uk
website: www.jbp.co.uk

The UK Vaping Industry Association is a leading trade organization that comprises some of the UK's fastest growing independent electric cigarette businesses, tobacco, and pharmaceutical companies.

Bibliography

Books

Elissa Bass, *E-Cigarettes: The Risks of Addictive Nicotine and Toxic Chemicals.* New York, NY: Cavendish Square Publishing, LLC, 2015.

Allan M. Brandt, *The Cigarette Century.* New York, NY: Basic Books, 2007.

Herbert Brean, *How To Stop Smoking.* New York, NY: Vanguard Press, 1951.

Eric Burns, *The Smoke of the Gods: A Social History of Tobacco.* Philadelphia, PA: Temple University Press, 2007.

Allen Carr, *Stop Smoking and Quit E-Cigarettes.* London, UK: Arcturus Publishing, 2014.

Jean-François Etter, *The Electronic Cigarette: An Alternative to Tobacco?* Scotts Valley, CA: CreateSpace, 2013.

Konstantinos E. Farsalinos et al., *Analytical Assessment of e-Cigarettes: From Contents to Chemical and Particle Exposure Profiles.* Amsterdam, NL: Elsevier, 2016.

Eric A. Feldman and Ronald Bayer, *Unfiltered: Conflicts over Tobacco Policy and Public Health.* Cambridge, MA: Harvard University Press, 2004.

Victor Fields, *Electronic Cigarette: The Beginners Guide to E-cigarettes, Vaping & E-hookah.* Scott's Valley, CA: CreateSpace, 2016.

Freshstart: 21 Days to Stop Smoking. New York, NY: The American Cancer Society, 1986.

Jane Friedman, *E-Cigarettes: Can the Electronic Devices Curb Tobacco Use?* Washington, DC: CQ Press, 2014.

Brett Kelly, *The Art and Science of Vaping: A Beginner's Guide to Electronic Cigarettes.* Seattle, WA: Amazon Digital Services, 2014.

Richard Klein, *Cigarettes Are Sublime.* Durham, NC: Duke University Press Books, 1995.

National Academies of Sciences, Engineering, and Medicine, *Public Health Consequences of E-Cigarettes.* Washington, DC: National Academies Press, 2018.

Robert L. Rabin and Stephen D. Sugarman, *Regulating Tobacco.* Oxford, UK: Oxford University Press, 2001.

Clete Snell, *Peddling Poison: The Tobacco Industry and Kids.* Santa Barbara, CA: Praeger, 2005.

US Department of Health and Human Services, *How Tobacco Smoke Causes Disease: The Biology and Behavioral Basis for Smoking-Attributable Disease: A Report of the Surgeon General.* Washington, DC: Office of the Surgeon General, 2010.

Christine Wilcox, *E-cigarettes and Vaping.* San Diego, CA: ReferencePoint Press, 2016.

The World Bank, *At What Cost? The Economic Impact of Tobacco Use on National Health Systems, Societies and Individuals.* Washington, DC: International Development Research Center, 2003.

Periodicals and Internet Sources

"AAFP, Others Applaud Surgeon General's Report on E-Cigarettes," American Academy of Family Physicians, December 12, 2016. https://www.aafp.org/news/health-of-the-public/20161212sgreporte-cigs.html.

Zachary Cahn and Michael Siegel, "Electronic Cigarettes as a Harm Reduction Strategy for Tobacco Control: A Step Forward or a Repeat of Past Mistakes?" *Journal of Public*

Health Policy, February 2011. https://link.springer.com/article/10.1057%2Fjphp.2010.41.

Priscilla Callahan-Lyon, "Electronic Cigarettes: Human Health Effects," *Tobacco Control*, May 2014. https://tobaccocontrol.bmj.com/content/23/suppl_2/ii36.

K. Michael Cummings and Robert N. Proctor, "The Changing Public Image of Smoking in the United States: 1964–2014," American Association for Cancer Research, January 2014. https://www.ncbi.nlm.nih.gov/pmc/articles/PMC3894634/.

Duncan Forgan, "Does Vaping Increase Your Risk of Heart Problems?" *Research the Headlines*, February 7, 2017. https://researchtheheadlines.org/2017/02/07/does-vaping-increase-your-risk-of-heart-problems/.

Rajeev K. Goel, "Smoking Prevalence in the United States: Differences across Socioeconomic Groups," *Journal of Economics and Finance*, April 2008.

Rachel A. Grana, Stanton A. Glantz, and Pamela M. Ling, "Electronic Nicotine Delivery Systems in the Hands of Hollywood," *Tobacco Control*, November 2011. https://tobaccocontrol.bmj.com/content/20/6/425.

Nathalie Gylling Hansen, "Cloud Gazing from Afar: A Comparative Analysis of How Electronic Cigarettes Are Branded and Perceived Across Markets," July 15, 2015. http://studenttheses.cbs.dk/handle/10417/5692.

Robert Lee, "Current Issues Regarding E-Cigarettes," American Psychiatric Association, November 2016. https://ajp.psychiatryonline.org/doi/pdf/10.1176/appi.ajp-rj.2016.111004.

Michael McCarthy, "Youth Exposure to E-Cigarette Advertising on US Television Soars," *British Medical Journal*, June 2014. https://www.bmj.com/content/348/bmj.g3703.

Jim McDonald, "Why American Vapers Should Say No to (Most) Medical Studies," *Vaping360*, July 23, 2017. https://vaping360.com/vape-news/51669/junk-vaping-science/.

Mark G. Myers and John F. Kelly, "Cigarette Smoking among Adolescents with Alcohol and Other Drug Use Problems," *Alcohol Research*, Fall 2006. https://www.ncbi.nlm.nih.gov/pmc/articles/PMC1931414/.

Sharon M. Nickols-Richardson, "Smoking Prevention: The Impact of Shock and Sap Appeal," *Journal of Family and Consumer Sciences*, November 2002.

Jonathan K. Noel, Vaughan W. Rees, and Gregory N. Connolly, "Electronic Cigarettes: A New 'Tobacco' Industry?" *Tobacco Control*, January 2011. https://tobaccocontrol.bmj.com/content/20/1/81/.

Janet Raloff, "Teen Vaping Soars Past Cigarette Use," *Science News for Students*, April 28, 2016. https://www.sciencenewsforstudents.org/article/teen-vaping-soars-past-cigarette-use.

W. Kip Viscusi and Jahn K. Hakes, "Risk Beliefs and Smoking Behavior," *Economic Inquiry*, January 2008.

N. A. Watson, J. P. Clarkson, R. J. Donovan, and B. Giles, "Filthy or Fashionable? Young People's Perceptions of Smoking in the Media," Oxford University Press, October 1, 2003. https://academic.oup.com/her/article/18/5/554/614590.

Olga Yevtukhova, "The Food and Drug Administration Kicks the Habit—The FDA's New Role in Regulation of Tobacco Products," *American Journal of Law & Medicine*, 2009.

Index